Where Is the Church?

To: Dong.
It is a blessing to see you at ABSW
as a student. And I wish all the best
in the wonderful things God has planned for you.
I am excited for you my brother

Dr. Ronald Burris

Where Is the Church?

Martyrdom, Persecution, and Baptism
in North Africa from the Second to the Fifth Century

RONALD D. BURRIS

Foreword by J. Rebecca Lyman

RESOURCE *Publications* · Eugene, Oregon

WHERE IS THE CHURCH?
Martyrdom, Persecution, and Baptism in North Africa
from the Second to the Fifth Century

Resource Publications
An Imprint of Wipf and Stock Publishers
199 W. 8th Ave., Suite 3
Eugene, OR 97401
www.wipfandstock.com

ISBN 13: 978-1-60899-808-1

Manufactured in the U.S.A.

*This book is dedicated to the students
at the American Baptist Seminary of the West
in Berkeley, CA, where I have the privilege of teaching
what I love: Church history.*

Deo gratias / Thanks be to God!

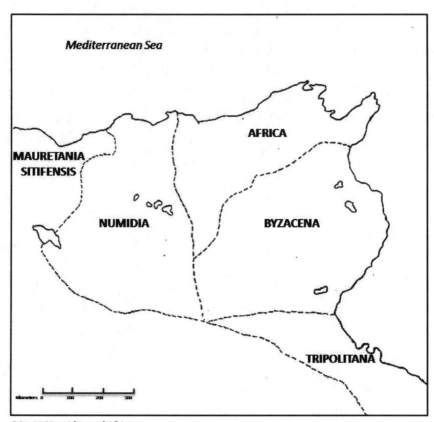

Map 1 Numidia and Africa

Contents

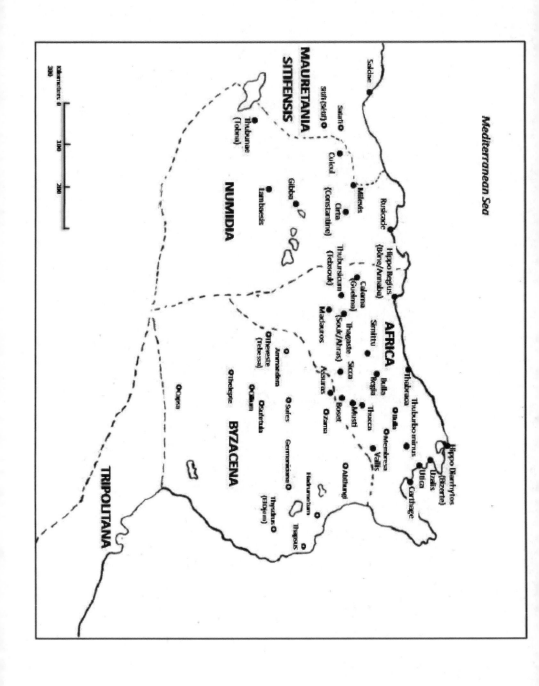

Foreword

OVER THE PAST DECADES the study of ancient Christianity has expanded to include not only a variety of new methodologies, but also the re-examination of those groups who were marginalized for political or theological reasons by the orthodox tradition. This narrative of the history of the Christian church in North Africa brings together older and newer scholarship to portray the particular theological and spiritual foundations of Christianity in Africa. As in other places around the Mediterranean, Christianity flourished in urban centers in relation to local culture as well as the Roman Empire. Ironically, these very ways of being Christian eventually came into conflict with other ways of being Christian as the church in the fourth and fifth centuries became a unified institutional body. The series of creeds and councils were only the organized markers of cultural transitions and religious compromises of Christians united by imperial policy and intense belief.

Remembered as the "Donatists," the century-long opponents of Constantine and then Augustine, the North Africans developed a rich theology of community, Holy Spirit, and martyrdom. Unimpressed by the growth of the imperial church under the patronage of the emperor, these Christians struggled to remain faithful to their own ancient tradition and life forged in conflict with Roman power. Dr. Burris sets out for us in sympathetic detail their struggles, their rich theology, and their lives. As a result we can better understand the authenticity of various forms of Christianity and the Church not only in the past but in our present day.

J. Rebecca Lyman

Acknowledgments

This work represents years of study and major revisions to a dissertation completed at the Graduate Theological Union in Berkeley, California in 2002. Of course this book would not have been possible without the help and encouragement of many family and friends, too numerous to name here. However, I would like to give a special thanks to my place of employment, the American Baptist Seminary of the West, for allowing me a sabbatical to complete this project. I would also like to thank Henry Millstein for his work in editing and his useful suggestions in helping me improve this work. In addition, I owe a debt of gratitude to Professor Maureen Tilley for taking time out of her busy schedule to read this manuscript. I do ask forgiveness, however, in not making all the recommended changes, but her encouragement and suggestions were invaluable. Also, I want to thank my mentor and friend Professor J. Rebecca Lyman for not only pushing me to begin this project but also helping me through its completion. Professor Lyman, you are a gift to the Body of Christ. Thank you very much! Finally, I take full responsibility for the contents in this book.

Abbreviations

MOST OF THE ABBREVIATIONS of titles of Greek and Latin works are
taken from *The SBL Handbook of Style*.

ANF	*The Ante-Nicene Fathers*
Apol.	*Apologeticus*
Bapt.	*De baptismo* [Tertullian]; *De baptismo contra Donatistas* [Augustine]
Carm.	*Carmina*
Ep	*Epistulae*
Gesta	*Gesta collationis Carthaginensis*
Hist. eccl.	*Historia ecclesiastica*
Hist. rom.	*Historia romana*
Laps.	*De lapsis*
LCL	Loeb Classical Library
Mart.	*Ad martyras*
Mort.	*De mortibus persecutorum*
NPNF	*The Post-Nicene Fathers*
Paen.	*De paenitentia*
Perp.	*Passio sanctarum Perpetuae et Felicitatis*
Petil.	*Contra litteras Petiliani*
PL	Patrologia Latina
Praescr.	*De praescriptione haereticorum*
Retr.	*Retractiones*
Schis.	*De schismate Donatistarum*
Scil.	*Passio sanctorum Scillitanorum*
Tral.	*Ad Trallianos*
Unit. eccl.	*De catholicae eccesiae unitate*
Vir. ill.	*De viris illustribus*
Virg,	*De virginibus velandis*

Introduction

THE SCHOLAR R. A. Markus inspired this work. In his book *The End of Christianity*, Markus offered the reader a more balanced perspective on the teaching and thought of Pelagius by placing him within the religious and social context of his day and asking the question Markus believed was on the minds of many fourth and fifth century Christians: "What does it mean to be an authentic Christian?" By doing this Markus demonstrated how many Christians during the late fourth century tried to answer this question as they wrestled with a profound identity crisis caused by the transformation of Christianity from persecuted sect to imperial religion. Many men and women, including Jerome and the monks who went out into the desert, thought the proper answer to the question was to live a life of perfection. Pelagius attempted to bring this traditional moral demand into the center of the city and the new Christian aristocracy. Augustine's defense of grace and "Christian mediocrity" had societal as well as theological stakes as the ascetic movement and imperial patronage transformed Christian laity and clerical authority in the fifth century. Thus, the Pelagian controversy represented the struggles of many Christians, and his teachings cannot be judged merely by pointing out that he was condemned by Augustine and several church councils. Markus challenged his readers, therefore, to reflect on theological controversies as part of a social transition to understand their ancient legitimacy in context.

Similarly, by asking the question "Where is the church?" I hope to place the Donatist controversy within the traditions of North African Christians facing a profound political and religious transformation, especially with their defense of the sacrament of water baptism and of martyrdom as baptism in blood. By providing a contextual overview of this controversy, I hope to show the reader why the majority of Christians in North Africa were drawn to this group. They continued the tradition that was bequeathed to them from the Scillitan martyrs, Tertullian, and their hero and martyr Saint Cyprian. They saw the true church as the church of the martyrs and the place where a proper baptism was administered. Their persistence as a community and their continuing elaboration of their theology, despite years of persecution and condemnation from their rivals, speaks to their commitment to those beliefs as defining the true church.

In chapter 1, I begin by giving an overview of North Africa (the Maghrib) before the Christian era. During this time (814 BCE—146 CE) North Africa went through several changes, as Carthage became the dominant trading center, competing with Greece for maritime dominance. In time, however, Carthage clashed with Rome in three Punic wars that resulted in a new height in Roman dominance. Towards the beginning of the Christian era, other areas of North Africa, Numidia and Mauretania, came under Roman control; yet within a century of the Roman conquest of Africa, Africans begin to influence Rome. Some scholars have called this the Africanization of Rome.[1]

In chapter 2, I examine in detail three versions of martyrdom: the accounts of the Scillitan martyrs and of Perpetua and Felicitas and their comrades, and Tertullian's letter of exhortation, *Ad Martyras,* to a group awaiting martyrdom. These accounts give a good idea of the type of Christianity that had taken root in North Africa. In the face of death as they defied the command to deny Christ, these Christians boldly stated: *Christianus sum*—"I am a Christian."

In chapter 3, I examine Tertullian's writings to understand him as a person and as an apologist and to show how he laid the theological foundation for North African Christianity, particularly in relation to the sacrament of baptism, the rebaptism of heretics, and martyrdom as a second penance.

In chapter 4, I begin by examining what we know of Cyprian from his writings and how the African church through the elaboration of ministerial offices had grown into a well-organized institution carrying out various ministries in the community. I then shift my focus to the issue of martyrdom (baptism in blood) to show how the Decian persecution forced Cyprian and other leaders to rethink the question: "Where is the Church?" I trace Cyprian's efforts to answer this question, giving special attention to his pastoral work *De lapsis.*

1. Wilhite, *Tertullian*, 30.

In chapter 5, I shift my focus from the baptism in blood to the sacrament of water baptism. The divisions that ensued from the Decian persecution challenge us to expand our question to "Where is the church and who are its members?" Is the church with the lapsed? Is it with the confessors only? And who has the authority to decide? I examine Cyprian's grappling with these questions in his letters and his major treatise *De ecclesiae catholicae unitate.*

Chapter 6 examines the devastating effects that Diocletian's persecution had on the Roman and North African churches. Old issues about baptism and discipline, which had been dormant since the Decian persecution, were brought to the forefront, causing the Roman and African churches to divide. Moreover, the church in North Africa divided into two separate churches as each group sought to define what constituted membership in the true church. These conflicts developed in the context of the rise of imperial Christianity and a Christian emperor, Constantine, who was willing to intervene in church disputes. As a result, church leaders began siding with secular powers to persecute other Christians.

In chapter 7, I discuss the general history of the period from 361–398, with special emphasis on the theological advances made by the Donatist bishop Parmenian. Because of the success of the Donatist Church, Parmenian had to deal with various schisms and the acknowledgement of sinners within the ranks of the true church. In addition, I examine Augustine's work *De baptismo*, in which he attempts to refute the Donatists' teaching on baptism and their claim to Cyprian's authority.

Chapter 8 examines the Donatists' last attempt to regain their status and power after the fall and execution of the chieftain Gildo and Bishop Optatus. In addressing this challenge they were led by one of their most able bishops up to that point, Bishop Petilian. I examine two of his most significant letters and the exchange between him and Augustine.

In chapter 9, I discuss the efforts by the Catholics to have the Donatists outlawed in two legislative acts. First, in 405 CE (Edict of Unity) the Catholics were able to have current heresy laws against the Manicheans applied to the Donatists. Second, in 411 CE, the Catholics succeeded in having Emperor Honorius call a universal African conference with the express intent of condemning the Donatists. After their condemnation, however, Donatist bishops still maintained that they were the true church. In particular, Bishop Petilian insisted that the transcript of the proceedings be fully documented so that future generations could decide who they believed represented the true church in North Africa.

In chapter 10, I give an overview of the entire book and suggest that the African idea of the church and its relationship to key doctrines such as baptism and the concept of *origo* explain why the majority of Christians in North Africa were attracted to Donatist teaching. I conclude that the reason for this is twofold: first, the Donatists built upon the African traditions that were articulated by Tertullian and continued by their beloved hero and martyr Saint Cyprian; and second, the native North Africans believed the Donatist Church more correctly represented what constituted the true church than did the Donatists' Catholic rivals. Thus it is understandable that in the face of imperial sanctions and severe persecutions the Donatist Church endured even beyond its condemnation by the Carthaginian Conference of 411.

1

North Africa before the Christian Era

THE AFRICAN SCHOLAR G. Mokhtar divides the territory of North Africa, the non-Phoenician inhabitants of the Maghrib, into three main areas. In the west, between the Atlantic and Lulucca is the territory known as Mauretania, inhabited by the Mauri people. In between the people of Mauri and the maximum western extension of the Carthaginians inland were the Numidae people, with their territory being Numidia. The third group was the Gaetuli, the nomads along the northern fringes of the Sahara.[1] However, when the Phoenician traders from Tyre begin to arrive on the coast of North Africa they found that area already inhibited by Libyans, whose language and culture survived well into the Roman period.[2] The Phoenicians did not come to make war with these native peoples but to establish ports for their trading endeavors. It has been suggested that the Phoenicians may have had ports every thirty miles or so to anchor their ships. Quite naturally, some of these ports would develop into permanent settlements, and three of their most important settlements were Carthage (f. 814 BCE) and Utica (f. 1101 BCE) in North Africa and Motya in Sicily. Mokhtar also emphasizes that all of the Phoenician settlements in North Africa and elsewhere were small settlements with not more than a few hundred people at most. As a result, the native peoples and the Phoenicians together were referred to as Punic by the Romans and Libyophoenicians by the Greeks.[3]

1. Mokhtar, *Civiliations*, 246.

2. Rives, *Religion*, 15.

3. Mokhtar, *Civilizations*, 248 Mokhtar also points out that the name Carthage in Pheonician is *Kart Hadasht*, meaning "New City," perhaps suggesting that Carthage was initally designed to be the Phoenicians' chief city. Polybius, *Rise of the Roman Empire*, 3.33 refers to the Carthaginian calvary as Libyan and Libyophoenician.

During the sixth century BCE Carthage became independent of Tyre and emerged as the leader of other Phoenician cities in North Africa. Over time, Punic Carthage also became a maritime power competing and eventually warring with Greece over the trading rights in Sicily. In 580 BCE Carthage succeeded in preventing the Sicilian Greeks from settling in North Africa by expelling them from the Punic settlements at Motya and Palermo. Later a Spartan named Dorieus tried to establish a settlement in Libya, but, with the help of the native Libyans, the Carthaginians were able to drive the Greeks out of Africa.[4] For four centuries Carthage and Greece fought battle after battle in the open seas, Carthage trying to maintain her trading dominance in western Sicily and the Greeks determined to get their fair share of trade.

THE WARS BETWEEN CARTHAGE AND ROME

Since Rome initially had no fleet and no commercial interest in the western Mediterranean, Rome and Carthage were on good terms for two centuries, signing treaties in 504 and 348 BCE. Yet events not of their making eventually caused both powers to clash in the first of three Punic wars that ultimately led to Carthage's destruction. Around 288 BCE, the city of Messana (modern Messina), under threat from Greek mercenaries, appealed to both Carthage and Rome for help. At the time, Carthage controlled large parts of Spain and was master of the islands in the Sardinian and Tyrrhenian Seas,[5] Rome feared that if Carthage got control of Messana, it could use this site to launch an attack on Italy; and so after a long debate, the Roman Senate agreed to help the Messanians.

After twenty-four years of fighting, during which Rome not only built a navy but also developed new techniques of naval warfare, the first war between Rome and Carthage came to an end in 241 BCE with a treaty requiring the Carthaginians, among other things, to pay a large indemnity. Unfortunately, subsequent events led to another war between these two powers. Immediately after the war ended, Carthage suffered from internal strife. Because the war was so costly, the government of Carthage could not pay their mercenaries, many of whom were native Libyans. A civil war ensued, and it was two years before Carthage could put down the insurgents. During this time, Rome took advantage of the

---

4. Mokhtar, *Civilizations*, 248.

5. Polybius, *Rise of the Roman Empire*, 1.10.

situation, seizing Sardinia and adding another 1,200 talents to the indemnity the Carthaginians were already required to pay. This action naturally inflamed Carthaginian hostility to Rome.[6]

For the next twenty-three years there was peace between Rome and Carthage, but the balance of power had shifted to Rome. The Carthaginians had lost their supremacy at sea as well as their holdings in Sardinia, Corsica, and Sicily. To counter its losses, Carthage rebuilt its empire by conquering large territories in Spain. Rome, on the other hand, continued its military conquests by winning several battles against the Gauls, a Celtic people that they had been fighting for over a century. The Carthaginian general Hamlicar directed the operations in Spain and became very adept at winning the respect and cooperation of the Celtic people there. His son Hannibal, who won the command of the Carthaginian army in 229 BCE, also had this gift, inspiring a multiracial army to fight under his command in the midst of tremendous hardships.

From several years of fighting in Spain, Hannibal and his troops were a cohesive fighting unit. As a result, they began seizing towns near Saguntum and in 229 BCE attacked Saguntum itself. This was a violation of the treaty Carthage had signed with Rome and led directly to a war that raged for almost three decades, during which Hannibal invaded Italy with his famous elephants. Ultimately, however, Rome prevailed with the help of Numidian troops.

Under the terms of the treaty ending this war Carthage had to give up most of its fleet, its elephants, and its prisoners of war. It also had to pay reparations, could not make war outside of Africa, and could make war in Africa only with Rome's permission.

Carthage survived and prospered for another fifty years, making every effort to be faithful to its treaty with Rome and even aiding Rome in wars against the Greek kings Philip and Antiochus. But Carthaginian prosperity made some in Rome nervous. One senator in particular, named Cato, ended every speech he gave on the Senate floor with the declaration *Carthago delenda est* ("Carthage must be destroyed").[7] Around the same time, King Masinissa of Numidia, who had made common cause with Rome, kept intruding into Carthaginian territory, claiming more than seventy towns. When the Carthaginians complained to Rome about this

---

6. Polybius, *Rise of the Roman Empire*, 3.10.

7. Plutarch, *Cato*, 27.

intrusion, Rome did nothing. Thus, in 150 BCE Carthage declared war on Masinissa and was defeated, violating their agreement not to make war in Africa without Rome's approval. As a result, Rome demanded that the Carthaginians do the impossible: leave their capital and move inland. When Carthage refused, Rome declared war on Carthage in 149 BCE. The Punic city held out for three years, but in 146 BCE the Romans razed it to the ground and ceremonially cursed it. Not all the citizens of Carthage were killed, however, nor did Punic culture come to an end. Mokhtar describes the situation after the sack of Carthage in 146 BCE:

> Rome only took over a small part of north-eastern Tunisia after the destruction of Carthage, and even this was largely neglected. In the rest of North Africa she recognized a series of client kingdoms which were generally left to their own devices. Within these kingdoms the cultural influence of Carthage continued and even increased as the older coastal settlements continued to flourish and many refugees from the last years of Carthage's struggle fled there. The Phoenician language in its later form known as Neo-Punic spread ever more widely.[8]

THE WAR BETWEEN NUMIDIA AND ROME

Rome's victory in the Punic Wars did not end the expansion of Roman power in North Africa. Masinissa was not happy with Rome's conquest of Carthage, since it precluded Numidia's seizure of the city and its territory, but he continued as an ally to Rome until his death in 148 BCE. His son Micipsa succeeded him and continued his good relations with the Empire, allowing his adopted son Jugurtha to assist Scipio Africanus[9] in Rome's war with Numantia. In this endeavor, Jugurtha won the respect of the Roman general Scipio and many men in Rome's army. When the war ended, Scipio sent a letter to King Micipsa praising the courage of Jugurtha and thanking him for his service.

Jugurtha, however, intriguing against Micipsa's natural sons for the Numidian throne, ultimately turned against Rome and waged a long and bitter war against his former ally until he was betrayed by Bacchus, the ruler of Mauretania, who in return for the favor received territory east

---

8. Mokhtar, *Civilizations*, 258.

9. The Roman general Scipio was given the name Scipio Africanus after his defeat of the great Carthaginian general Hannibal.

of Moulouya. Rome then put another descendant of Masinissa on the throne. Masinissa's line continued to rule Numidia until one of his descendants sided with Pompey in Rome's first civil war. After Pompey's defeat by Caesar at Thapsus in 46 BCE, Rome ruled Numidia directly.[10] The province created by Caesar was called Africa Nova. The other province to make up the Roman *proconsularis* was called Africa Vetus. This consisted of Carthage and the other territories conquered by Rome during the third Punic war.

THE LAND OF MAURETANIA

Information concerning the Mauretanian kingdom is meager in comparison to that concerning Numidia and Carthage. King Bogud II supported Caesar against Pompey in Rome's first civil war and so had his territory expanded into parts of Numidia. In Rome's second civil war between Mark Antony and Octavian, Bogud II supported Mark Anthony, while Bocchus II, a rival for the Mauretanian throne, chose the winner, Octavian. As a result, Bogud II was driven out of his territory and Bocchus II took his place. Bocchus II died in 33 BCE, and there was no ruler in the area until Augustus in 25 BCE installed Juba, son of the last Numidian king. Juba grew up in Rome from the age of four and was highly educated, writing several books in Greek that are now lost.[11] He ruled the territory for 40 years as a loyal client of Rome and was succeeded by his son Ptolemaus, who ruled until he was executed by the emperor Gaius in 40 CE. After his execution, Mauretania was divided into two provinces, completing the organization of the Maghrib or North Africa under Roman rule.

NORTH AFRICA UNDER ROMAN RULE

The native people experienced both hardship and benefits from Roman rule. On the one hand, the Roman elite and veterans carved out large estates in Africa, reducing farmlands for the natives and diminishing areas traditionally roamed by the nomads. As a result, many native tribes rebelled, and the Roman government was never able to fully control the region. On the other hand, many natives were able to move up the social ladder and become a part of elite Roman society. In fact, over time Africans began to influence Roman politics and other areas of Roman life.

10. Mokhtar, *Civilizations*, 258.

11. Ibid., 259.

By 170 CE, the number of African senators had increased to around one hundred, the largest group after the Italians.[12] Wilhite comments:

> Well into the second century, a shift occurred where the trend of Rome influencing Africa was reversed, and Africa began to influence Rome. Raven explains, "For most of the second century [the Africans] were to dominate the intellectual life of the Empire, and by the 180s nearly a third of the Roman Senate was of African origin." Moreover, in 193 (and until 211) Lucius Septimius Severus became the first African emperor of Rome, followed by his two sons, Geta and Caracalla. Whereas the first period of Roman presence in Africa could be described as the Romanization of Africa, the latter period could conversely be labeled the Africanization of Rome.[13]

This complex and tumultuous mix of peoples and cultures decisively influenced the history that is the main topic of this book: the growth, development, and influence of Christianity in North Africa.

Rome's ability to conquer so many different tribes and peoples of the ancient world allowed it to build the greatest empire of the ancient world and indeed one of the greatest in human history. Yet Christianity was able to capture, if not conquer, both the inhabitants of the Roman Empire and its conquerors, the Germanic tribes of Europe. But how did they accomplish this feat? Not with the sword, but with an unshakable faith in their God, even in the face of death; and nowhere perhaps was this unshakeable faith more fiercely demonstrated than in North Africa. To this strange group of people we shall now turn.

---

12. Mokhtar, *Civilizations*, 276.

13. Wilhite, *Tertullian*, 30.

2

Martyrdom and the Church in North Africa

THE SCILLITAN MARTYRS /
PASSIO SANCTORUM SCILLITANORUM

SCHOLARS HAVE NOT DETERMINED with any certainty when and how Christianity arrived in North Africa.[1] Acts 2:1-12 tells of the apostles speaking in the languages of various peoples throughout the empire, including the language of Libya. So it is quite possible that converts from this experience were inspired to carry the gospel back to Africa and other parts of the empire, although this cannot be proven.[2] Since Carthage was a major harbor, it is also quite possible that Christian traders introduced Christianity from other parts of the empire during the first century as they moved about exchanging goods and ideas, but this cannot be proven either.[3] Perhaps Margaret Miles summed it up best: "The origins of North African Christianity are lost in obscurity."[4]

It is certain, however, that by the late second century Christianity was flourishing in North Africa and reaching many converts among the native population. The first recorded evidence of a Christian community dates from 180 CE; the first known North African bishop is Agrippinus.[5]

---

1. Paul Monceaux, who wrote seven volumes on the literature of African Christianity, offers several theories on the origin of North African Christianity, but concludes with the following: "Nous ne savons rien de précis sur l'évangélisation de l'Afrique." Monceaux, *Histoire,* 1:3.

2. Professor Timothy David Barnes considers this a possibility. He offers less support, however, for the view that the Carthaginian Christian community owes its origin to the Carthaginian Jewish community around 150. Barnes, *Tertullian,* 64.

3. For a more recent overview on the various theories concerning the origin of Christianity in North Africa, see Dunn, *Tertullian,* 13–18.

4. Miles, *Spirituality,* 351.

5. Cyprian, *Ep.* 71.4.

Significantly, our earliest record of North African Christinity is a martyrdom account, that of the Scillitan martyrs, so named from the city
of Scillium.[6] On July 16, 180, twelve African Christians were accused
of Christianity by the newly elected proconsul Vigellius Saturninus,
and from the account of their trial we get a good idea of the type of
Christianity that had taken root in the area. In the face of death, these
seven men and five women refused to submit to the authorities' demands.
When Speratus, one of the twelve, was asked to swear by the genius of our
Lord the Emperor, he boldly declared: "I do not recognize the empire of
this world; but rather I serve that God, whom no man has seen nor can
see with these eyes."[7] Speratus insisted that he was a good citizen; he told
his interrogator that he did not steal and that when he purchased anything, he made sure to pay the tax. Nonetheless, he insisted that the only
Lord he could acknowledge was the one that is over both emperor and
nations. When asked if he wanted to reconsider his position, he repeated
the popular statement *Christianus sum* ("I am a Christian"). The other
eleven also held firm in their faith and were all sentenced to death by the
sword. When the proconsul Saturninus pronounced their sentence, they
all said *Deo gratias* ("thanks be to God"), another phrase that would soon
become a popular slogan among African Christians. Lastly, when their
fate appeared certain, Nartzalus said, "Today we are martyrs in heaven.
Thanks be to God!"[8] The martyrs' resolve to opt for persecution in the
face of death left a lasting impression on North African Christianity.[9] As
Timothy Barnes notes, the *Passio sanctorum Scillitanorum* attests not only
to the penetration of Christianity into the countryside of North Africa
but also to the fact that these Christians were willing to reject what they
believed was an alien world for the rewards of heaven.[10] Moreover, the
existence of the Scillitan martyrs as a determined group ready to die for
the faith and the fact that they had in their possession portions of the

6. The text and translation used here are from Musurillo, *Acts*, 86–89.

7. *Scil.* 15.6: "Ego imperium huius seculi non cognosco; sed magis illi Deo servio
quem nemo hominum vidit nec videre his oculis potest."

8. *Scil.* 25.15: "Hodie martyres in caelis sumus. Deo gratias."

9. *Scil.* 25.16 gives the names of the seven men and five women who were the first
Christian martyrs of Africa that we know of: Speratus, Nartzalus, Cittinus, Veturius,
Felix, Aquilinus, Laetantius, Ianuaria, Generosa, Vestia, Donata, and Secunda.

10. Barnes, *Tertullian*, 62–3.

Latin Bible[11] suggest that the Christian community at Scillium had come into existence years before this encounter, perhaps as early as 150. Finally, although it is difficult to indicate the precise location of the martyrs' hometown, Christianity did indeed flourish there, for at the Conference of Carthage in 411 both Catholics and Donatists produced bishops (*episcopi Scillitani*) from that town.

THE MARTYRDOM OF PERPETUA AND FELICITAS / *PASSIO SANCTARUM PERPETUAE ET FELICITATIS*

In 203, just twenty years after the Scillitan martyrdoms, another group of African Christians proved willing to die for their faith. The episode is depicted in the *Passio sanctarum Perpetuae et Felicitatis,* most of which is presented as a first-person narrative by Perpetua; it is extant in both a Latin and a Greek version.[12] This is the story it narrates: when ordered to offer sacrifice for the welfare of the emperors, Revocatus, Felicitas, Saturninus, Secundulus and Vibia Perpetua refuse. At the time of their arrest, Felicitas is eight months pregnant, and Perpetua, a wellborn married woman, is nursing her newborn child. Soon after their arrest, Perpetua's father comes to her to convince her to recant her beliefs. Perpetua realizes that although her father's actions and words stem from his love for her, he does not understand what she has become. To help him understand, she offers a simple but profound comparison, asking her father to look at a vase in the room where they are gathered. Then she asks her father if that vase or water pot can be called by any name other than what it is. When he says no, she replies, "Well I too cannot be called anything other than what I am, a Christian."[13] At these words her father leaves in anger. When he has gone, she gets herself baptized and is inspired by the Holy Spirit not to ask for any special treatment but simply to persevere to the end (3.5). Nonetheless, deacons from her community, Tertius and Pomponius, intervene by bribing the soldiers into moving the prisoners into a section of the prison with better accommodations. As a result, Perpetua is allowed not only to nurse her baby but also to be with him

11. When the proconsul Saturninus asked them 'What do you have in your case?" Speratus responds, "Books and letters of a just man Paul" ("libri et epistulae Pauli viri iusti," *Passio* 5.15). The martyrs had personal possession of some scripture, apparently some of Paul's letters, but they are not more specific than this.

12. The text and translation used here are from Musurillo, *Acts*, 106–31.

13. *Perp.* 3.2: "Sic et ego aliud me dicere non possum nisi quod sum, Christiana."

for an extended period (3.9). To these blessings, she says, "My prison had suddenly become a palace, so that I wanted to be there rather than anywhere else."[14] Heffernan and Shelton compare the Latin and Greek texts at this point (3.5) and note that the Latin text uses the word *recipimur* ("we are received"), while the Greek text uses the more violent word ἐβλήθημεν ("we were thrown").[15] Since Latin is probably Perpetua's native language and she appears to be careful in the words she uses to describe her ordeal, Heffernan and Shelton suggest that this Latin word speaks of the martyrs' desire or willingness to receive (*recipere*) martyrdom. Moreover, the declaration by Perpetua that her prison had become a palace (*praetorium*) fits this wording, since one is received (*recipimur*) into a palace and not thrown there.[16]

As the martyrs continue in their ordeal, it becomes apparent not only that Perpetua is the leader of the group but also that she has received special powers from the Lord. Consequently, her brother Saturus, eager to know their fate, asks her to seek a vision from the Lord telling whether she (and the others by implication) would be condemned or freed (4). Perpetua, also believing that she had the right to seek God for such a thing, made her request and immediately experienced a vision: she saw a ladder that one could climb all the way to heaven, but only with great care because there were sharp objects that would cut and mangle the careless climber. Moreover, at the base of the ladder lay a large dragon whose job it was to scare anyone who dared take the first step. Saturus successfully climbs the ladder first and as he reaches the top, he yells back to warn her of the dragon. Perpetua, however, finds a weapon that renders the dragon frightened and helpless. With confidence she declares that "in the name of Jesus Christ"[17] she will not be bitten. After this declaration she steps upon the head of the dragon who now fears her (4.7). She reaches the top and is welcomed by a white-haired man in shepherd's clothing who is surrounded by thousands of people in white garments. The white-haired man gives her some milk to drink. After she drinks the milk, the white-robed multitude says, "Amen." At the sound of this word, she awakens with a sweet taste in her mouth. She and her brother discuss the vision

14. *Perp.* 3.9: "et factus est mihi carcer subito praetorium, ut ibi mallem esse quam alicubi."

15. Heffernan and Shelton, "Paradisus in carcere," 219.

16. Ibid., 220.

17. *Perp.* 4.6: "in nomine Jesu Christi."

and conclude: "We realized that we would have to suffer, and that from now on we would no longer have any hope in this life."[18]

After this vision, Perpetua and her companions are informed that they will be having a hearing in a few days. Her father also knows of this hearing, so he again pleads with Perpetua to reconsider her position. Now, however, their relationship has changed. Her father no longer addresses her as *filia* (daughter) but with the more respectful *domina* (lady, mistress) (5.5). In the role reversal intimated by this change of language, her father throws himself to the ground, kisses her hand, and cries aloud as he pleads with her to consider how her martyrdom is going to hurt her family. Perpetua, probably emboldened by her recent dream, tries to get her father to understand the issue: "I tried to comfort him saying; It will all happen in the prisoner's dock as God wills; for you may be sure that we are not left to ourselves but are all in his power."[19] In other words, if God wills her to die as a martyr, it will be well, for God's power will sustain her. Many Christians before and after Perpetua have realized that martyrdom is a gift from God and that no person can endure such a trial on his or her own. Often in my teaching duties at the Baptist seminary in Berkeley, California, I hear a student say, "Man, I could never have been a martyr"—to which I reply, "That is exactly the point. You cannot endure martyrdom in your own strength; the power of God must be with you." Realizing that they have received the gift of martyrdom, Perpetua and her companions again refuse the governor's order to sacrifice on behalf of the emperors. Hilarianus, the newly elected governor, sentences them to death by the wild beasts. At the announcement of their sentence, they are all overjoyed (6.6).

As they wait for their day in the arena, Perpetua's deceased brother Dinocrates is brought to her mind. As she contemplates the terrible death he suffered while alive, she realizes that in her present position she can pray for him (7.2). She begins to do so in earnest. That same night she has a vision of Dinocrates, seeing him in a place of suffering. When she awakens she finds new assurance: "I was confident that I could help him in his trouble and I prayed for him every day until we were transferred

18. *Perp.* 4.10: "et intelleximus passionem esse futuram, et coepimus nullam iam spem in saeculo habere."

19. *Perp.* 5.6: "et confortavi eum dicens: Hoc fiet in illa catasta quod Deus voluerit. Scito enim nos non in nostra esse potestate constitutos, sed in Deo."

to the military prison."[20] Judith Perkins makes an insightful observation about this episode:

> This dream displays Perpetua's recognition of a difference between pagan and Christian suffering. Dinocrates' plight in the afterlife is offered in terms resembling Perpetua's experiences in prison. Both endure heat, dirt, and suffering; she is confident she can help her brother. She believes her suffering in prison has earned her favor and influence with the deity.[21]

A second dream confirms her belief: she sees Dinocrates clean, well dressed, and healed of his earthly wound. He drinks from a golden bowl that remains full and after he has drunk his fill, he begins to play. As she awakens, Perpetua realizes that her brother has been delivered from his suffering (8). The conclusion is clear: while Dinocrates' suffering merited him nothing but pain on earth and in the afterlife, the suffering of Perpetua, coupled with her prayers, wins him release from both his pain and his place of torment.[22]

As Perpetua and her companions approach the day of their martyrdom, Perpetua notices that her guard Pudens begins to show them great honor, "realizing that we possessed some great power within us."[23] Referring to the day before the martyrdom, the narrator states, "by this time the adjutant who was head of the jail was himself a Christian."[24] It is certainly possible that the narrator is talking about the conversion of Pudens, who began showing Perpetua and her companions great honor as he witnessed their steadfast faith in the face of death. The case for such an interpretation is strengthened by the words spoken to Pudens by Saturus. Before the latter's martyrdom he exhorts the adjutant as if trying to convince him either to receive the faith or to be strong in the faith that he has already received: "It is exactly as I foretold and predicted. So far not one animal has touched me, So now you may believe me with all your heart; I am going in there and shall be finished off with one bite of the

---

20. *Perp.* 7.9: "sed fidebam me profuturam labori eius et orabam pro eo omnibus diebus quousque transivimus in carcerem castrensem."

21. Perkins, *Suffering Self,* 108.

22. Ibid., 109.

23. *Perp.* 9.1: "intellegens magnam virtutem esse in nobis."

24. *Perp.* 16.4: "iam et ipso optione carceris credente."

leopard."[25] The phrase "believe with all your heart" certainly may imply that Pudens is already a believer whose faith needs strengthening. Saturus believes, as Tertullian will later, that his martyrdom itself and the fact that it happened as he predicted were good reasons to become a Christian and "believe with all one's heart." For not only does Saturus die by one bite from the leopard as he predicted, but the crowd, without knowing it, gives witness to this baptism by blood; at the sight of such bloodshed the spectators shout, "Well washed! well washed!" (21.2; *Salvum lotum! salvum lotum!*). Before Saturus dies, he encourages Pudens one more time to remember the faith, and then he takes Pudens' ring and dips it in his blood as a pledge and as a record of his bloodshed.[26]

The martyrdom of the others is also depicted as marked by dramatic effect and divine intervention. For example, Saturninus wants to be exposed to several animals that his crown may be all the more glorious (19.4), and he receives his request. On the other hand, Saturus, discussed above, fears being attacked by a bear and wants to be killed by one bite of the leopard, and this is granted. Moreover, at the time of their arrest Felicitas, eight months pregnant, is saddened by the possibility that she would miss the opportunity to be martyred with her comrades because Roman law prohibits the execution of pregnant women (15.2). However, after intense prayer by the entire group, her baby is delivered early.

At the delivery of her child, she is heard crying out at the pains of childbirth. Upon hearing her cries, a prison guard reminds Felicitas of the more excruciating pain she will feel when the wild beasts attack her in the arena. To this she replies, "What I am suffering now, I suffer by myself. But then another will be inside me who will suffer for me, just as I shall be suffering for him."[27] Events as depicted in the *Passio* prove her right. After her baby girl is born, Felicitas hands her over to a sister in the community to raise as her own (15.7). At the appointed time she goes into the arena and receives her crown. Felicitas and the other martyrs know that martyrdom is a gift from God and that God will see them through their ordeal.

---

25. *Perp.* 21.1: "Certe, sicut praesumpsi et praedixi, nullam usque adhuc bestiam sensi, et nunc de toto corde credas; ecce prodeo illo, et ab uno morsu leopardi consummor."

26. *Perp.* 21.5: "pignus relinquens illi et memoriam sanguinis." On the day of the martyrdom, many in the crowd are reported to have believed, but we are not given any number.

27. *Perp.* 15.6: "Modo ego patior quod patior, illic autem alius erit in me, qui patietur pro me, quia et ego pro illo passura sum."

The account of Perpetua's martyrdom teaches the same lesson. Before she can receive her final test, her father comes to make one last appeal to change her mind. This time he pulls out his hair from his beard and throws it to the ground; finally he throws himself to the ground. Her father appears to be the only one among her kin who does not understand her martyrdom. Earlier in the narrative, Perpetua says concerning him, "I was sorry for my father's sake, because he alone of all my kin would be unhappy to see me suffer."[28] From this statement, it appears that her other family members, though saddened by their impending loss (3.8–9), are not unhappy with her decision to stand strong in her faith. The reason is probably that they are Christians who understand that martyrdom is a gift from God, whereas her father, an unbeliever, does not.

The day before she fights the wild beasts in the arena, Perpetua receives her third and final vision: she is bought into the arena and ordered to fight against an Egyptian with a "vicious appearance." If he wins, he can kill her with the sword, and if she prevails she will win the golden wreath. Before the battle begins, Perpetua is miraculously transformed into a man and as a man she wins the fight. The crowds go wild as they shout and sing the psalms along with her assistants. She then walks over to accept the branch of victory, along with which she receives a kiss and words of comfort: "Peace be unto you, daughter."[29] When she awakens, she realizes the meaning of her dream: the wild beasts ordered by Hilarianus will not kill her, and her fight is not against men but against the devil.

From here the narrator tells of her final victory. Before entering the arena the prisoners are forced to wear the apparel of the Roman gods. The men put on the robes of Saturn and the women the dress of Ceres, but Perpetua vehemently refuses to comply. The official gives in to her demands. Next they are stripped naked, at which the crowd exhibits so much displeasure that they are brought back out of the arena. Finally Perpetua and her companions enter the arena in tunics. Perpetua is heard singing the psalms with a shining countenance. The crowd sees them as condemned criminals, but the narrator, speaking for their Christian community, sees Perpetua "as the beloved of God" (18.2; *ut Dei delicata*) and "as a wife of Christ" (18.2; *ut matrona Christi*). In her first contest, Perpetua does battle with a heifer. When attacked by the beast she is

28. *Perp.* 5.6: "et ego dolebam casum patris mei quod solus de passione mea gavisurus non esset de toto genere meo."

29. *Perp.* 10.13: "filia, pax tecum."

knocked down, her tunic is torn, and she becomes disoriented. Because she is "in a state of ecstasy of the spirit," she does not feel the pain.[30] At a moment of rest she asks, "When are we going to be thrown to that heifer or whatever it is?"[31] When she is told that this episode has already occurred, she cannot believe it until she examines her torn tunic and the bruises on her body. The words spoken earlier by Felicitas have come to pass for Perpetua: "another will be inside me who will suffer for me, just as I shall be suffering for him."[32] Before being killed by the sword and not by the beasts—just as foretold by her vision—she encourages the remaining martyrs with these final words: "You must all stand fast in the faith and love one another, and do not be weakened by what we have gone through."[33] As Perkins notes, "Perpetua's narrative has explicitly conveyed her courage, toil, endurance. The martyrs' *Acts* depict martyrs rejecting the victim's role by their subtle collapsing of the athlete's code. They hold that to die is to win; the wreath is death. Death itself becomes in Christian terms the victory."[34]

TERTULLIAN TO THE MARTYRS / *AD MARTYRAS*

Tertullian, who was probably a young adult at the time of the martyrdoms at Scillium, writes to another group of martyrs around 202. In his letter *Ad martyras* Tertullian encourages these confessors to remain faithful. We are not told of their execution date, but from the contents of the letter we can assume that it is imminent. With such an urgent situation at hand, Tertullian not only exhorts them to remain faithful but also offers several examples showing how and why they should do so. Tertullian exhorts: "First, then O blessed, grieve not the Holy Spirit, who has entered the prison with you. For if he had not gone with you there, you would not have been there this day. And do give all endeavor, therefore, to retain him; so let him lead you thence to your Lord."[35] To reach their

---

30. *Perp.* 20.8: "adeo in spiritu et in extasi fuerat."

31. *Perp.* 20.8: "Quando, inquit, producimur ad vaccam illam nescioquam?"

32. *Perp.* 15.6: "autem alius erit in me qui patietur pro me, quia et ego pro illo passura sum."

33. *Perp.* 20.10: "In fide et invicem omnes diligite, et passionibus nostris ne scandalizemini."

34. Perkins, *Suffering Self*, 111.

35. *Mart.* 1.3: "Inprimis ergo, benedicti, nolite contristare Spiritum sanctum, qui vobiscum introiit carcerem. Si enim non vobiscum nunc introisset, nec vos illic hodie

goal, Tertullian insists the confessors must rely on the Holy Spirit who gave them this gift of martyrdom in the first place; they can then be assured that they will be led to the Lord. Tertullian also admonishes them to consider their new abode as a place of retirement and the world that they left as the real prison (2.1), because the secular world is a prison of many temptations for the Christian. For example, in the world one will be tempted to look on strange gods, one will be influenced to participate in pagan holidays, public shows, brothels, and much more. But now in their present condition the prison can be for the Christians what the desert was for the prophets. Echoing what Perpetua had said earlier, Tertullian concludes this exhortation by saying, "let us drop the name prison; let us call it a place of retirement."[36] In the meantime, Tertullian advises them to deal with their present situation by focusing on the Holy Spirit and thereby allowing the Spirit to take them to a realm beyond physical pain:

> Though the body is shut in, though the flesh is confined, all things are open to the spirit. In sprit, then, roam abroad; in spirit walk about, not setting before you shady paths or long colonnades, but the way which leads to God. As often as in spirit your footsteps are there, so often you will not be in bonds. The leg does not feel the chain when the mind is in the heavens. The mind compasses the whole man about, and whither it wills it carries him. But where your heart shall be, there shall be your treasure.[37]

Because the Holy Spirit is present to assist believers, complete reliance and meditation on the Holy Spirit, in Tertullian's view, will not only sustain confessors but also bring them to a place of peace in their present suffering. Nonetheless, not to appear insensitive or unreasonable, Tertullian does admit, "Grant now O blessed, that even to Christians the

---

fuissetis. Et ideo date operam ut illic vobiscum perseveret et ita vos inde perducat ad Dominum." The translation is from Evans, ANF 3.

36. *Mart.* 2.8: "Auferamus carceris nomen, secessum vocemus."

37. *Mart.* 2.9–10: "Etsi corpus includitur, etsi caro detinetur, omnia spiritui patent. Vagare spiritu, spatiare spiritu, et non stadia opaca aut porticus longas proponens tibi, sed illam viam, quae ad Deum ducit. Quotiens eam spiritu deambulaveris, totiens in carcere non eris. Nihil crus sentit in nervo, cum animus in caelo est. Totum hominem animus circumfert, et quo velit transfert. Ubi autem erit cor tuum, illic erit et thesaurus tuus."

prison is unpleasant. But yet we were called to the warfare of the living God in our very response to the sacramental words."[38]

After making this admission, Tertullian encourages the confessors and future confessors by offering them examples of heroes and heroines that have endured pain "for the sake of fame and glory."[39] In a display of historical knowledge, Tertullian mentions the following persons: Lucretia, the virtuous Roman wife who killed herself because her honor had been violated:[40] Mucius, a Roman of noble birth who displayed contempt of torture by placing his right hand in the fire and defying the pain;[41] Heraclitus, a Greek philosopher who covered himself with warm manure and died: Empedocles, a Greek who leaped into the fire at Aetna;[42] and Peregrinus, a Cynic philosopher who jumped into the funeral pyre at the Olympic Games in 165 BCE. He then cites three African women of distinction who for love of country and honor ended their own lives: Queen Dido, the founder of Carthage,[43] the wife of the Carthaginian command-

---

38. *Mart.* 3.1: "Sit nunc, benedicti, carcer etiam Christianis molestus, vocati sumus ad militiam Dei vivi iam tunc, cum in sacramenti verba respondimus."

39. *Mart.* 4.3: "famae et gloriae causa."

40. Not only was Lucretia a women of character and chastity, but her suicide spurred the revolution that overthrew the tyrannical rule of Lucius Tarquinius Superbus and ushered in the Roman republic. Zoch, *Rome*, 29–31. The story is told in Livy 1.58–59.

41. When Rome was at war with the Etruscans, Gaius Mucius got permission from the Senate to assassinate the Etruscan king, Porsenna. In his attempt, however, he killed the wrong person and was threatened with being burned alive. In defiance of this threat, he placed his hand in the fire to show he had no fear of death. At this, Porsenna let him go. In return, Mucius told the king the Roman plan of attack. Porsenna was so moved by Mucius's action that he sought peace with Rome. Zoch, *Rome*, 42–44. The original source is Livy 2.12–13.

42 The philosopher Empedocles is said to have died by leaping into the flames of Mt. Aetna to prove his divinity. Sacks, *Greek*, 88. Cf. Diogenes Laertius 8.2.67–69.

43. According to Vegil's epic poem *The Aeneid*, Dido, the queen of Carthage, and Aeneas, the future founder of Rome, fall in love. They plan to get married until the god Mercury reminds Aeneas that it is his duty and destiny to found a territory that would later become the Roman Empire. His departure breaks Dido's heart. She commits suicide as he is sailing away, but before she dies she curses Aeneas and his descendants (*Aen.* 4.622–27). Vergil attributes the Punic wars to this curse. Zoch, *Rome*, 7–8. Although Dido's story is fictional, Augustine reports in his *Confessiones* 1.21 that he wept when he read of the betrayal of Dido.

er Hasdrubal,[44] and Cleopatra .[45] Finally, he pays tribute to Regulus,[46] the famous Roman general who chose to be given back to the Carthaginians and suffer death rather than betray his oath to them (4.6), and to the Spartan youth, who are encouraged to endure pain in the presence of their parents and relatives (4.8).

One might wonder why Tertullian does not cite Christian martyrs, especially since the New Testament and Africa provide such splendid— and undoubtedly well-known— examples of martyrs' endurance. But his point is very clear: if the persons he names could endure such pain for worldly fame and glory (4.3), then how much more should the Christian endure pain since "we are called to the warfare of the living God."[47] Moreover, if what the unbelievers did has the value of glass, then surely the Christian's sacrifice has the value of a genuine pearl (4.9; *si tanti vitreum, quanti verum margaritum*). And most importantly, if the unbeliever can do these heroic deeds for what is false, then how much more should Christians suffer for what is true (4.9)? David E. Wilhite suggests that in this exhortation to women Tertullian is criticizing Rome:

> Tertullian's list of martyrs is antagonistic towards Rome in that it glorifies women who have subverted Rome's oppression and who are, therefore, positive examples of martyrdom. Tertullian displays these women in contrast to the 'hysterical men' who died for *gloria,*

44. When Carthage was finally taken by the Roman general Scipio (146 BCE), the city was set on fire; Hasdrubal begged for mercy from Scipio, but his wife, scorning her husband, killed her two sons and from the top of the burning temple of Eshmoun threw them and herself into the flames. Appian, *Hist. rom.* 8.19.130–31.

45. With the death of Cleopatra's lover Anthony, her efforts to save Egypt from Roman domination definitively failed, so she killed herself. Her death was a courageous act because it allowed her to keep her honor once she lost her country. The Roman poet Horace pays tribute to her courage in *Carm.* 1.37.21–32: "Seeking to die honorably, she had no coward's fear of the sword, nor did her swift fleet make for hidden shores. Her face serene, she dared to behold her helpless palace, brave enough even to clutch deadly snakes so she could take the black poison into her body. All the more fierce—she planned her own death—she deprived Caesar's swift Liburnian ships of her being led in his proud triumph like a meek woman." Zoch, *Rome,* 222–26.

46. During the first Punic war, the Carthaginians captured the Roman commander, M. Atillius Regulus. They allowed him to return under escort to Rome but made him promise to negotiate the release of their prisoners or have Rome agree to their terms of peace. Placing his country above his own life, he persuaded the Roman Senate to refuse their offer. He returned to Carthage and was tortured to death. Zoch, *Rome,* 97–98.

47. *Mart.* 3.1: "Vocati sumus ad militiam Dei vivi."

which gives this "religious" tract a political element which is contextually charged for Carthaginian women awaiting persecution.[48]

In his conclusion, Tertullian reminds the confessors that in everyday life people suffer abuse and even torture at the hands of criminals with no good purpose in mind and endure such abuses with no assistance from anyone. The martyrs of Christ, on the other hand, suffer, as Tertullian has previously pointed out, because they are the "blessed elect" of God, and the Holy Spirit guides and strengthens them, for they are nourished by the breast of our Lady, Mother Church.[49]

Throughout this short tract, Tertullian speaks to the would-be martyrs as if they will indeed succeed in winning the martyr's crown. For technically one is not a martyr until one has died for the faith. Persons who suffer but survive their ordeal are called confessors. Yet Tertullian never refers to these believers as confessors. He begins his tract by calling them "blessed martyrs" (1.1) who are in their present position because the Holy Spirit has guided them to that place. They are therefore the elect of God, chosen to receive the gift of martyrdom. Tertullian's task is simply to help the martyrs realize the gift that God has already given them.

Tertullian's teaching and North African Christianity generally show an emphasis and reliance on the Holy Spirit and the church as "mother" whose breast strengthens the believer in times of adversity. Martyrdom is inseparable from the relationship of the believer to the Holy Spirit and the church. For one cannot receive the call to martyrdom without being chosen by the Holy Spirit, nor can the believer endure this trial without the nourishment of Mother Church.

PERSECUTION AND CHRISTIANS IN THE ROMAN EMPIRE / *TERTULLIAN THE APOLOGIST*

In addition to the threat of persecution, Tertullian understood that he had to defend the very image of Christians within the Roman Empire. Consequently, his biggest challenge was to make Christianity understood and appreciated by the inhabitants of the empire. At the same time, he had to demonstrate to the public that Christians could be good citizens with-

---

48. Wilhite, *Tertullian*, 167.

49. *Mart.* 1.1: "Inter carnis alimenta, benedicti martyres designati quae vobis et domina mater ecclesia de uberibus suis et singuli fratres de opibus suis propriis in carcerem subministrant."

out worshipping the Roman gods or participating in the imperial cult. In the second and third century, however, being a Christian was thought so diametrically opposed to being a good Roman that Tertullian faced a difficult, if not impossible, task. In a society where the Roman gods were seen as the protectors and guarantors of Roman peace and security and the emperors were invested with divinity, Christians' insistence on not serving the imperial ruler of the world was truly revolutionary.[50] As Evans notes, they were not revolutionary because they tried to overthrow the Roman government; they did not. They were revolutionary because they were committed to a way of life in which both the presuppositions and the practical working out of their faith were at radical variance with the norms and practice of Roman life.[51]

As a result, there was a clash between social orders. In response to these dissident Christians, Roman emperors staged large civil events where "the torture and death of martyrs and other criminals showed forth for all to see the vanquishing and destruction of those who refused to conform in the society."[52] In his *Apologeticus*, Tertullian appeals to non-Christians, arguing that the Romans misuse their own laws and persecute Christians without any valid evidence. Tertullian insists that Christians are accused of many violations and that when they are arrested, they are denied justice. He maintains that the reason for this injustice is ignorance; the public at large does not understand Christians. Having presented his case, he asks a biting question: "This, then, is the first grievance we lodge against you, the injustice of the hatred you have for the name of Christian. The motive that appears to excuse this injustice is precisely that which both aggravates and convicts it; namely, ignorance."[53]

Not only does Tertullian insist that Christians are unjustly hated, but he also exposes what he believes to be the reason for this hatred: imperial Rome is afraid of the rapid growth of Christianity. For once people learn

---

50. Evans, *One and Holy*, 5–7.

51. Ibid., 5.

52. Perkins, *Suffering Self*, 117. Concerning martyrdom as a social display, Perkins notes how the martyrdom of Perpetua and her companions was scheduled during the official military games held to honor the birthday of Geta, the son of emperor Septimius Severus.

53. *Apol.* 1.4-5: "Hanc itaque primam causam apud vos collocamus iniquitatis odii erga nomen Christianorum. Quam iniquitatem idem titulus et onerat et revincit qui videtur excusare, igorantia scilicet." Cf. Sider, *Christian and Pagan*, 9.

who Christians truly are, they will not only respect them but also want to join their ranks:

> The proof of their ignorance is this: in the case of all who formerly indulged in hatred because of their ignorance of the nature of what they hated, their hatred comes to an end as soon as their ignorance ceases. From this group come the Christians; and Christians are really as numerous as you allege us to be. People cry that the state is besieged, that Christians are in the country, in the villages, on the islands; men and women, of every age, of every state and rank of life, are transferring to this group, and this they lament as if it were some personal injury. In spite of this fact, people's minds are not directed to the consideration of some underlying good.[54]

Tertullian insists that despite persecution the church is reaching many converts from all walks of life. Since he is obviously writing as an apologist for Christianity, we must cautiously examine his claims. While we can be fairly certain that at that time Christianity throughout the empire was on the rise, we do not know whether its growth was as rapid as he says.[55] Nonetheless, this growth (whatever its size) certainly included persons from all walks of life and was probably of some concern to the imperial authorities in Africa, perhaps in a manner similar to that which led Pliny to raise several questions about Christians with the emperor Trajan around 111. Since authorities could not easily tolerate Christians' refusal to participate in the imperial cult, martyrdom, as Tertullian asserts in several of his writings, was to be expected.[56] For this reason, it is not surprising that Tertullian in several of his letters spends much time preparing believers for what he thought would be their greatest challenge.

---

54. *Apol.* 1.6–8: "Testimonium ignorantiae est, quae iniquitatem dum excusat, condemnat, cum omnes qui retro oderant, quia ignorabant quale sit quod oderant, simul desinunt ignorare, cessant et odisse. Ex his fiunt Christiani, utique de comperto, et incipiunt odisse quod fuerant, et profiteri quod oderant, et sunt tanti quanti et denotamur. Obsessam vociferantur civitatem; in agris, in castellis, in insulis Christianos; omnem sexum, aetatem, condicionem, etiam dignitatem transgredi ad hoc nomen quasi detrimento maerent. Nec tamen hoc modo ad aestimationem alicuius latentis boni promovent animos." Cf. Sider, *Christian and Pagan*, 9–10.

55. Concerning the growth rate of Christianity during the early period there is modern evidence to suggest that Tertullian may not have been exaggerating at all. For example, Rodney Stark estimates the growth of Christianity at 40 percent for the first several centuries. This is based upon Stark's work with the Mormon Church. Stark, *Rise*, 6–7.

56. Only the Jews, because of their ancient history, were allowed to worship freely without offering sacrifices to the Roman gods. Pagels, *Eve*, 49.

Moreover, when Christians did suffer martyrdom, the accounts of these incidents were passed around various Christian communities, making the martyrs heroes and heroines.

Judith Perkins, however, insists that these texts did more than just make martyrs famous. In her view, they helped Christians throughout the empire gain an understanding of themselves as persons willing and ready to suffer. Tertullian, she writes, "described a code that facilitated martyrdoms: If he (a Christian) is denounced, he glories in it, if he is accused, he does not defend himself, when he is questioned, he confesses without any pressure, when he is condemned, he renders thanks."[57] By analyzing the early martyrs throughout the empire, Perkins suggests that Christians' attitudes toward suffering and martyrdom were a part of their ethos and worldview. Consequently, Christian martyrs should not be considered abnormal, for in their context "their aspirations were not only normal but also normative."[58] She also notes that the imperial authorities were well aware of Christians' desire to suffer and often criticized them for this impulse, on a few occasions releasing them precisely to thwart it.[59] Tertullian in his closing exhortation cites this dilemma:

> In that case, you say, why do you complain of our persecutions? You ought rather to be grateful to us for giving you the suffering you want. Well, it is quite true that it is our desire to suffer, but it is in the way that the soldier longs for war. No one indeed suffers willingly, since suffering necessarily implies fear and danger. Yet, the man who objected to the conflict both fights with all his strength and when victorious, rejoices in the battle, because he reaps from it glory and spoil.[60]

Tertullian likens the Christian to a reluctant soldier who must do his duty, insisting that no Christian wants to suffer, but is like a soldier who, though afraid, fights with all his strength once engaged in a battle. When

---

57. Perkins, *Suffering Self*, 31, referring to Tertullian, *Apol.* 1.12.

58. Ibid., 33.

59. Ibid., 22. Perkins maintains that Christians were known more for their willingness to suffer death than for miracles.

60. *Apol.* 50.1–2: "Ergo, inquitis, cur querimini quod vos insequamur, si pati vultis, cum diligere debeatis per quos patimini quod vultis? Plane volumus pati, verum eo more, quo et bellum miles. Nemo quidem libens patitur, cum et trepidare et periclitari sit necesse. Tamen et proeliatur omnibus viribus, et vincens in proelio gaudet qui de proelio querebatur, quia et gloriam consequitur et praedam."

the battle is won, the soldier rejoices over worldly spoils; in a similar but more glorious manner, the Christian is summoned to the tribunal to fight, but fights for the truth, for "this victory has attached to it the glory of pleasing God and the reward of eternal life."[61] For when the Christian is killed, at the very moment when the authorities think they have the victory, Tertullian insists, "we conquer in dying."[62]

But there is more. Before concluding his treatise, Tertullian cites the same long list of pagan heroes and heroines (with a few additions) that he cited in his letter *Ad Martyras* and finishes: "We become more numerous every time we are hewn down by you: the blood of Christians is seed."[63] In a powerful literary device, Tertullian declares the imperial persecution ineffective, for its attempt to destroy Christianity had in fact caused Christians to multiply like a harvest.

Nonetheless, martyrdom could be a problem for the church as well as a blessing. Because martyrdom could bring forgiveness of any post-baptismal sins, many sought martyrdom as a way of receiving both forgiveness and a certain degree of fame. In addition, other Christians began to believe that their sins could be forgiven if a confessor simply prayed for them. As a result, no sooner were confessors incarcerated than members of the church began viewing them as spiritual heroes. Consequently, many Christians (even in Tertullian's time) began seeking their advice. More alarming still, some Christians began seeking their prayers for the forgiveness of certain sins in lieu of completing the prescribed penance. As a result, future confessors and martyrs would affect the doctrine of the church as it related to the authority of the bishop and the practice of penance. Moreover, martyrdom would forever leave its imprint on the North Africans' understanding of what it meant to be the true church. Many North African Christians as late as the fourth and fifth centuries would maintain that the true church was a persecuted church, the church of the martyrs.

61. *Apol.* 50.2: "Ea victoria habet et gloriam placendi deo et praedam vivendi in aeternum." Cf. Sider, *Christian and Pagan*, 69.

62. *Apol.* 50.3: "Ergo vicimus, cum occidimur."

63. *Apol.* 50.13: "Plures efficimur quotiens metimur a vobis; semen est sanguis Christianorum."

3

Tertullian: Baptism and the Church

TERTULLIAN THE MAN

FROM TERTULLIAN'S WRITINGS I now proceed to a consideration of Tertullian himself. In the closing lines of Tertullian's treatise on baptism (*De baptismo*), he refers to himself, saying, "This I pray, that as you ask you also have in mind Tertullian, a sinner."[1] The only other time Tertullian refers to himself in his writings, he adds his *gentilicium* (tribal name): "May peace and grace from our Lord Jesus Christ redound: as likewise to Septimius Tertullianus, whose this tractate is."[2] Concerning the tribal name of Septimius, Wilhite notes that the Septimii were predominantly of humble status in Tertullian's time, with the notable exception of those from Lepcis Magna, from which came the first Roman emperor of African descent, Septimius Severus (146–211).[3] Lepcis was one of the larger Punic cities of Tripolitania, but it appears that Tertullian was from Carthage. The African historian Optatus, writing around the time of Augustine, expressly states that Tertullian was a Carthaginian.[4] Jerome, who refers to the apologist as Tertullian the African, also believes that his birthplace is Carthage.[5] It is certainly possible, however, that a man with Tertullian's education was born in Lepcis but moved to Carthage where

---

1. *Bapt.* 20.5: "Tantum oro, ut cum petitis etiam Tertulliani peccatoris memineritis." Cf. Wilhite, *Tertullian*, 18.

2. *Virg.* 17.9: "Pax et gratia a domino nostro Iesu redundet cum Septimio Tertulliano, cuius hoc opusculum est." During the medieval period, his name appeared as Quintus Septimius Florens Tertullianus. Tertullian never referred to himself with all these names, but scholars have not rejected them. See Wilhite, *Tertullian*, 18.

3. Wilhite, *Tertullian*, 18.

4. Optatus, *Schis.* 1.8.

5. Jerome, *Vir. ill.* 53.1.

his talents could be better utilized and appreciated. If, then, there is some uncertainty where Tertullian was born, there is still more uncertainty when he was born and when and how he died. Furthermore, there was around the same time a lawyer in Rome with the same name. This fact has led some scholars to conclude that these two men were in fact the same person. Timothy Barnes, however, has soundly refuted this supposition as well as Jerome's suggestion that Tertillian's father was a centurion or a proconsul.[6] We know that Tertullian was married, for he wrote a work to his wife, *Ad uxorem*, discussing marriage as an idealized state where both parties live in perfect harmony and work together to serve God. We can also be certain that Tertullian was highly educated; thirty -one works of his in Latin are extant, while between fifteen and eighteen (including several in Greek) are lost.[7] Because of this enormous literary output, he is often called the "father of Latin Christianity." His first works can be dated around 197 and his latest around 212/213, although his treatise *On Modesty* (*De pudicitia*) has been dated as late as 220.[8]

It has commonly been believed both that Tertullian was an ordained presbyter and that he became a Montanist in his later years. Barnes, however, has made influential arguments against both these suppositions. On the latter point, Wilhite says, "Tertullian was simply the first great teacher of unimpeachable doctrinal orthodoxy who dared to enunciate an unpalatable truth: the church is not a conclave of bishops, but the manifestation of the Holy Spirit."[9] Even more pointedly, Dunn states, "No work of Tertullian is unorthodox. They may be unusual and extreme, but they are not heretical."[10] Tertullian certainly attacked some individuals in the church, but he did so as a member of the church.

In summary, Tertullian was a native Christian who benefited from Romanization, was married and well educated, lived a long productive life, and saw himself as a defender of the faith. Yet he was very critical of his opponents and particularly critical of Rome, because, as Wilhite suggests, he wrote with the self-identify of an African.[11]

6. Barnes, *Tertullian*, 1–30.
7. Dunn, *Tertullian*, 7.
8. Sider, *Christian and Pagan*, xi.
9. Wilhite, *Tertullian*, 24–25.
10. Dunn, Tertullian, 9.
11. Wilhite, *Tertullian*, 27.

TERTULLIAN, WATER BAPTISM AND CHURCH DISCIPLINE

Tertullian not only encouraged believers to remain faithful in the face of death but also instructed them how to live in a hostile environment. In his work *On the Shows* (*De spectaculis*), Tertullian explains to his fellow Christians what he believes to be the proper conduct for Christians in the Roman Empire. From his heated arguments against Christian attitudes toward the games, we can deduce that many Christians not only attended these shows on a regular basis but also felt there was no harm in doing so. Tettullian insists that this behavior is not "consistent with true religion, and true obedience to the true God."[12] But how does one determine what is true or appropriate behavior in such an environment?

Tertullian admits that there is no specific scriptural reference forbidding entering a circus or theatre or watching shows or combat, as is the case with other sins such as murder or idol worship that are mentioned specifically in Scripture. Nonetheless, Tertullian comes up with a creative argument: he challenges believers to look back on their baptism ceremony. In fact, his main argument against the shows is centered on the sacrament of baptism:

> But lest anyone suppose us to be quibbling, I will turn to authority, the initial and primary authority of our "seal." When we enter the water and profess the Christian faith in the terms prescribed by its law, we profess with our mouths that we have renounced the devil, his pomp, and his angels. What shall we call the chief and outstanding matter, in which the devil and his pomps and his angels are recognized, rather than idolatry? From which every unclean and evil spirit, I may say—but no more of that. So, if it shall be established that the whole equipment of the public shows is idolatry pure and simple, we have an indubitable decision laid down in advance that this profession of renunciation made in baptism touches the public shows too, since they, being idolatry, belong to the devil, his pomp, and his angels.[13]

12. 1.4: "Ista non competant verae religioni et vero obsequio erga verum deum." Text and translation of *De spectaculis* from Glover, LCL.

13. 4.1–3: "Ne quis argutari nos putet, ad principalem auctoritatem convertar ipsius signaculi nostri. Cum aquam ingressi Christianam fidem in legis suae verba profitemur, renuntiasse nos diabolo et pompae et angelis eius ore nostro contestamur. Quid erit summum atque praecipuum, in quo diabolus et pompae et angeli eius censeantur, quam idololatria? Ex qua omnis immundus et nequam spiritus ut ita dixerim, quia nec diutius de hoc. Igitur si ex idololatria universam spectaculorum paraturam constare constiterit,

Because Tertullian is confident that he can show the connection between shows and idolatry, he ends this section with a challenge: "If among
all these anything shall be found unconnected with an idol, we shall pro-
nounce it to have no bearing on idolatry, to have no connection with our
renunciation."[14] Tertullian refers here to the renunciation every Christian
makes at baptism, renouncing the devil and his works and accepting
Christ. As a result, the Christian is expected from that point forward to
live for Christ and should not even come close to doing something that
conflicts with the oath made at baptism. Tertullian thus reminds believers
not only of their baptism but also of what they confessed on that occasion. Tertullian calls the act of baptism the Christian's highest "seal" of
authority. For it is at baptism that one confesses the Christian faith; that
confession includes the renunciation of any form of idolatry. To make the
connection between idolatry and the shows, Tertullian surveys the history of the Roman games (*ludi*) to demonstrate that they are founded upon
idolatrous worship. Hence he warns believers that "by such acts [i.e., by
patronizing the shows] we really renounce and unseal the seal, by unseal-
ing our witness to it."[15] In other words, participation in the shows violates
the very oath one makes when entering the church through baptism. In
addition, Tertullian argues that rejection of these shows indicates to the
world that a person has adopted the Christian faith. Thus, his *De spectaculis* creatively uses the sacrament of baptism to teach church discipline.

TERTULLIAN AGAINST THE HERETICS

In his work *On the Prescription of Heretics* (*De praescriptione haereticorum*), Tertullian defends the church from certain heretics who, having
abandoned the rule of faith confessed at baptism, sought to destroy the
faith of believers. These heretical teachers of various gnostic persuasions
proved to be a serious threat to the early church. Because the faith of
many Christians (weak and strong) had been shattered, Tertullian sought
to spell out the essential beliefs of Christianity in opposition to the false
or misleading teachings of gnostics and various other teachers. In his

---

indubitate praeiudicatum erit etiam ad spectacula pertinere renuntiationis nostrae testimonium in lavacro, quae diabolo et pompae et angelis eius, scilicet per idololatrian."

14. 4.4: "Si quid ex his non ad idolum pertinuerit, id neque ad idoloatrian neque ad
nostram eierationem pertinebit."

15. 24.3: "Ceterum sic nos eieramus et rescindimus signaculum rescindendo testa-
tionem eius."

opening address he points out two facts. First, heresies undoubtedly exist, since Jesus himself spoke of them; second, even strong men at times accept false teaching. But this should not cause alarm, Tertullian continues, for Christians do not place their faith in people, whether they be bishops, deacons or virgins; rather "true faith" proves itself by perseverance: "no one is wise but the faithful, no one excels in dignity but the Christian; and no one is a Christian but he who perseveres even to the end."[16] In Tertullian's view, however, it is just as important to place one's faith in the correct teaching of the Church as it is to persevere. The problem with the heretics of his day was that they deceived others as well as themselves by choosing false teaching; and the main reason for this deception was that they were always inquiring into disputations and seeking deeper and deeper truth. In order to justify their inquiries, writes Tertullian, many of his opponents made use of Jesus' saying, "Seek and ye shall find" (Luke 11:9). After some discussion, he grants that this verse is directed to everyone and that all should seek the truth, but he adds that one cannot search for truth indefinitely; there should be a purpose and a limit to this search:

> You must seek until you find, and believe when you have found; nor have you anything further to do but to keep what you have believed, provided you believe this besides, that nothing else is to be believed, and therefore nothing else is to be sought, after you have found and believed what has been taught by Him who charges you to seek no other thing than that which He has taught.[17]

In their unrestricted seeking the heretics abandon the rule of faith that firmly establishes the sound doctrine upon which the church stands. Tertullian therefore carefully restates what that rule of faith is:

> Now with regard to this rule of faith—that we may from this point acknowledge what it is which we defend—it is, you must know, that which prescribes the belief that there is one only God, and that he is none other than the creator of the world, who produced all things out of nothing through his own Word, first of all sent

16. 3.6: "Nemo est sapiens nisi fidelis, nemo maior nisi christianus, nemo autem christianus nisi qui ad finem usque perseveraverit." Translation from Evans, ANF 3.

17. 9.4: "Unius porro et certi instituti infinita inquisitio non potest esse; quaerendum est donec invenias et credendum ubi inveneris, et nihil amplius nisi custodiendum quod credidisti, dum hoc insuper credis, aliud non esse credendum ideoque nec requirendum cum id inveneris et credideris quid ab eo institutum est, qui non aliud tibi mandat inquirendum quam quod instituit."

forth; that this Word is called his Son, and under the name of God, was seen "in diverse manners" by the patriarchs, heard at all times in the prophets, at last brought down by the spirit and power of the Father unto the Virgin Mary, was made flesh in her womb, and, being born of her, went forth as Jesus Christ; thenceforth he preached the new law and the new promise of the kingdom of heaven, worked miracles; having been crucified, he rose again the third day; (then) having ascended in to the heavens, he sat at the right hand of the Father; sent instead of himself the power of the Holy Spirit to lead such as believe; will come with glory to take the saints to the enjoyment of everlasting life and of the heavenly promises, and to condemn the wicked to everlasting fire, after the resurrection of both these classes shall have happened, together with the restoration of their flesh.[18]

In Tertullian's opinion this rule of faith defines and separates Christians from heretics. It not only comprises the basic tenets of Christian faith but also represents the tradition that existed since the apostles. Once we have discovered this tradition, we must stop seeking and begin walking according to the rule handed down by the apostles to the church. Moreover, Tertullian challenges the gnostics' claim that they are the true heirs of apostolic teaching and possess some secret knowledge. He first points out that they cannot show that their teachings are within the boundary of the rule handed down from the apostles; and then he challenges them to produce original records of their churches showing a connection of their bishops to the apostles. Concerning this second point, Tertullian introduces a concept into North African Christianity that would be taken up and adapted by later African writers. That concept was *origo*.

18. 13.1–5: "Regula est autem fidei, ut iam hinc quid defendamus profiteamur, illa scilicet qua creditur. Unum omnino Deum esse nec alium praeter mundi conditorem qui universa de nihilo produxerit per verbum suum primo omnium emissum. Id verbum filium eius appellatum in nomine Dei varie visum a patriarchis, in prophetis semper auditum, postremo delatum ex spiritu patris Dei et virtute in virginem Mariam, carnem factum in utero eius et ex ea natum egisse Iesum Christum. Exinde praedicasse novam legem et novam promissionem regni caelorum, virtutes fecisse, cruci fixum, tertia die resurrexisse, in caelos ereptum sedisse ad dexteram patris, misisse vicariam vim spiritus sancti qui credentes agat, venturum cum claritate ad sumendos sanctos in vitae aeternae et promissorum caelestium fructum et ad profanos adiudicandos igni perpetuo, facta utriusque partis resuscitatione cum carnis restitutione."

TERTULLIAN AND THE CONCEPT OF ORIGO

The concept of *origo* has to do with the source or the root of a thing, in other words, its beginning, which determines the class of things to which it belongs: "every sort of a thing must necessarily revert to its original for its classification."[19] As Merdinger shows, for Tertullian the concept of *origo* is related to his Trinitarian theology and his idea of the unity of the church.[20] The gnostics are from a source (*origo*) other than the one founded by Jesus and his apostles, thereby proving that they are outside the bounds of the church. While Cyprian and the Donatists would later adapt and use this concept for their own purposes, for Tertullian it is crucial in refuting the gnostics and other heretics: they cannot show a connection to the apostles through a succession of bishops, and their teaching also bears record that they are from another *origo,* for if they were of the same source they should have the same rule of faith. Tertullian is careful to note that, on the contrary, the churches in Africa, like the one in Rome, have the one apostolic *origo* because they, following in the tradition of the apostles, have the same rule of faith and honor the martyrs.

For Tertullian the rule of faith is more important than apostolic succession. He maintains that many churches are not derived from the direct line of an apostle but nonetheless have the same rule of faith, thus demonstrating that they are of the proper *origo*.

In summary, the key point in Tertullian's teaching on membership in the church is that a Christian must accept the rule of faith and must persevere in this teaching to the end. Tertullian uses the rule of faith both offensively and defensively. It both informs us who the true members of the church are and excludes those, such as gnostics, who are outside its boundaries. Those who are deemed its members drink in her faith, are sealed with the sacrament of baptism, blessed with the Holy Spirit, fed with the eucharist, and encouraged by the martyrs. And of such discipline, Tertullian asserts, the church admits no gainsayers.[21]

---

19. *Praescr.* 20.7: "Omne genus ad originem suam censeatur necesse est."

20. Merdinger, *Rome,* 38. Merdinger also notes that it was Brisson who first pointed out this concept in his *Autonomisme et christianisme.*

21. *Praescr.* 36.5: "et inde potat fidem; eam aqua signat, Sancto Spiritu vestit, eucharistia pascit, martyrium exhortatur et ita adversus hanc institutionem neminem recipit."

TERTULLIAN'S TREATISE ON BAPTISM

Thus far, I have discussed the sacrament of baptism in relationship to membership in the church. Tertullian also discusses the relationship of baptism to the rule of faith, teaching that one's belief in the rule is then sealed by the oath taken at baptism. Although one must persevere to the end in this faith, it is at baptism that one renounces the world and enters the church.

In Tertullian's treatise *On Baptism* (*De baptismo*) he treats the subject in some detail. Like many of his works, the treatise was motivated by the current problems within the church at Carthage. A certain woman of a sect called "Cainite" had lured away some members from the church with her false teaching. As a result, other members in the church raised questions that caused doubt among the simple. So it was necessary for Tertullian to review in detail the sacrament of baptism and its significance for the church. Tertullian charges his opponent with being a viper, creating a metaphor that sets his opponent in dramatic contrast to the true believer. For as vipers, he says, "frequent dry and waterless places," we (the true believers) are little fishes, and Jesus Christ is our great fish; like fish we receive in water the new birth.[22] Tertullian then explains the sacramental significance of water itself and how it was given special power to wash away sins. He reminds his readers that from the beginning of creation water held a special place over the other elements, because God chose water as the resting place of the Holy Spirit. Moreover, during the very act of creation water divided the firmament, and its withdrawal caused the dry land to appear. Water was also the first of the elements to produce living creatures, so "is it not a marvel that by the bathing of baptism death is washed away?"[23] For water was present in the clay that formed the first man, but it received its special powers by being the resting place of the Holy Spirit. Tertullian explains this by saying that a thing placed beneath another is bound to take onto itself the quality of that which is suspended over it; thus, water, being under the Holy Spirit, received power from the Spirit. In Tertullian's words:

---

22. 1.2–3: "in aqua nascimur." Translation from Evans, ANF. The reference to Jesus as "fish" undoubtedly stems from the early Christian use of Greek ιχθυς "fish" as an acronym for the Greek words for "Jesus Christ, Son of God, Savior."

23. 2.2: "Nonne mirandum est lavacro dilui mortem?"

> Thus the nature of the waters, having received holiness from the holy, itself conceived power to make holy. Let no one on that account object, "But are we then baptized in those same waters which were there in the beginning?" Not those very same—still the same, to the extent that the species is one.[24]

Because water has special power, Tertullian says that it makes no difference where one is baptized; whether it is the sea, a pond, a river or a fountain, it is all the same.

Here Tertullian introduces a concept that proved influential in later African Christianity: that of a "holy angel" acting on and through the baptismal water. After pointing out that "unclean spirits do settle upon waters, pretending to reproduce that primordial resting of the divine Spirit upon them [i.e., the waters],"[25] Tertullian argues that "no one should think it over-difficult for God's holy angel to be present to set waters in motion for man's salvation."[26] Tertullian attributes to this "holy angel," whom he compares to the angel who set in motion the waters at the pool of Bethsaida, "that cancelling of sins which is granted in response to faith signed and sealed in the Father and the Son and the Holy Spirit;"[27] the angel is a "type" or forerunner, as John the Baptist was forerunner to Jesus. This angel is clearly distinct from the Holy Spirit, since Tertullian considers that it cleanses the baptizands and makes them "ready for the Holy Spirit." Later African Christian writers were to take up this concept of a baptismal angel.

Another point articulated by Tertullian that would be very influential in African Christianity is his rejection of baptism performed by heretics. Tertullian insists that there is only one baptism, one church, and one God, and therefore he cannot imagine that a heretic has the right to scripture, the eucharist, or Christian baptism. Concerning this point, he states:

24. 4.1–2: "Ita de sancto sanctificata natura aquarum et ipsa sanctificare concepit. Ne quis ergo dicat, 'numquid ipsis enim aquis tinguimur quae tunc in primordio fuerunt?' Non utique ipsis, si non ex ea parte ipsis qua genus quidem unum, species vero complures."

25. 5.4: "immundi spiritus aquis incubant adfectantes illam in primordio divini spiritus gestationem."

26. 5.5: "Ne quis durius credat angelum dei sanctum aquis in salutem hominis temperandis adesse."

27. 6.1: "abolitione delictorum, quam fides impetrat obsignata in patre et filio et spiritu sancto."

Certainly we have justification for discussing what practice should be observed in respect of heretics. For it is to us the announcement was made; whereas heretics have no part or lot in our regulations: the very fact of their being deprived of fellowship bears witness that they are outsiders. It is no duty of mine to take cognizance in them of a precept enjoined upon me: they have not the same god as we have, nor have they the one that is the same, Christ; consequently they have not the one, because they have not the same baptism. And they have it not at all, and there is no possibility of enumerating a thing which is not in (any one's) possession.[28]

Tertullian argues that heretics have no right to Christian baptism for at least three reasons: 1) they are outside the church; 2) because their beliefs are different from those of the church, they worship a different god; and 3) their baptism is not done in proper form. I suggest that Tertullian is not being original here but is expounding what Christians in North Africa had already taught and believed. The evidence for this assertion is that Cyprian states that Bishop Agrippinus, Tertullian's predecessor, did not accept heretical baptism and consequently baptized or rebaptized those who entered the church from heretical groups. Because there was only one baptism, and heretics did not have it, the general North African practice was that persons baptized in heretical groups had to be baptized or rebaptized to enter the true church.

In addition to rejecting heretical baptism, Tertullian held that sins committed after baptism could place one outside the bounds of the church. Concerning this point Evans makes an insightful comment:

Tertullian . . . is a witness for a traditional rigorism, eschatological in its orientation, which tended to view the commission of sin after baptism as placing one outside the peace and communion of the Church. Three sins in particular, sins against God, were regarded as having this effect: idolatry, murder, and adultery. For Christians guilty of one of these there was the sole expedient of "second repentance," called also "confession," and by the Greek equivalent of the latter term, *exomologesis*. The sinner clothes himself in sackcloth and ashes, prostrates himself before both presbyters

28. 15.2: "Sed circa haereticos sane quae custodiendum sit digne quis retractet. Ad nos enim editum est: haeretici autem nullum consortium habent nostrae disciplinae, quos extraneos utique testatur ipsa ademptio communicationis. Non debeo in illis cognoscere quod mihi est praeceptum, quia non idem deus est nobis et illis, nec unus Christus, id est idem: ergo nec baptismus unus, quia non idem. Quem cum rite non habeant sine dubio non habent, nec capit numerare quod non habetur."

and people, and pleads for their intercession to God that he, the sinner, will be forgiven. This procedure issues not in restoration to communion in the church, but, as Tertullian reports, to virtual assurance that God will in the end forgive. In casting himself upon the prayers of the church the sinner is in fact entreating Christ, since "the church of Christ" and God will not fail to hear his Son.[29]

On this point of a "second repentance," Tertullian and the church at Rome were sharply divided. For Callistus, the bishop of Rome, had determined earlier that Christians who committed one of the "gross sins," adultery, could be readmitted to full communion of the church. Evans contends that it is this action that prompted Tertullian to write his angry treatise *On Chastity* (*De pudicitia*), in which he openly criticizes a certain bishop as the *pontifex maximus*[30] who dares to forgive sexual sins that only God can forgive. Scholars disagree as to the identity of this bishop. Some believe it was Tertullian's own bishop Agrippinus and others that it was Bishop Callistus of Rome. Merdinger takes the latter view and argues:

> It is not possible to be certain, given the paucity of evidence and Tertullian's characteristic terseness. Nonetheless, I prefer the traditional view that Tertullian's opponent is in fact the bishop of Rome. From an independent source (Hippolytus, a Roman theologian and contemporary of Tertullian) it is well known that Callistus inaugurates a new era in Rome, granting pardon to adulterers and revising the stance of his church on marriage with social inferiors.[31]

Both the Roman and African churches were receiving new members, and of course Tertullian and others saw this as good. But it was also a challenge to insist that believers have the level of commitment to live up to Tertullian's standards. Thus, for practical reasons, Bishop Callistus offered them forgiveness through penance. In Tertullian's view, this was unacceptable, because at that time persons who were baptized, having been washed clean, were expected to cease from sinning or at least to desist from committing any major sins. If they did not stop sinning, there was no recourse but to hope to receive the gift of martyrdom, a baptism

---

29. Evans, *One and Holy*, 35.

30. The *pontifex maximus* was the leading high priest for pagan rituals. Although the Roman church would later use this term of its own bishop, at the time Tertullian used it, he was, in my opinion, being sarcastic.

31. Merdinger, *Rome*, 32–33.

in blood. On this point, Tertullian states that "we have indeed a second washing, it too a single one, that of blood, of which our Lord said, 'I have a baptism to be baptized with,' when he had already been baptized. For he had come by water and blood, as John has written, so as to be baptized with water and glorified with blood."[32] The result, in Tertullian's view, is that this second baptism "makes actual a washing which has not been received, and gives back again one that has been lost."[33] In consonance with this view, Tertullian emphasizes the seriousness of the sacrament of baptism, arguing that "happy is that water which cleanses once for all, which is not a toy for sinners to amuse themselves with, and is not tainted with repeated application of filth, so as to defile once more those whom it cleans."[34] Therefore, baptism was a one-time act, and if one committed gross sins afterwards, only a baptism in blood could give back what had been lost. For this reason, Tertullian discouraged young people or children from getting baptized before they were ready, insisting that "deferment of baptism is more profitable in accordance with each person's character and attitude, and even age: and especially regarding children."[35]

Nonetheless, while Tertullian encouraged certain persons not to rush into baptism, he was also aware of the danger of the other extreme. Many in Africa and throughout Christendom would put off baptism until the end of their lives, often on their deathbed.[36] Tertullian addressed this problem in his work *On Repentance* (*De paenitentia*), in which he encourages novices to follow up repentance with baptism and a committed life. He urges, however, that if one chooses to wait, one must do one's best to serve God in the meantime. Cutting to the point, Tertullian charges that "people meanwhile steal the intervening time and make it for themselves

32. 16.1: "Est quidem nobis etiam secundum lavacrum, unum et ipsum, sanguinis scilicet, de quo dominus Habeo, inquit, baptismo tingui, cum iam tinctus fuisset. Venerat enim per aquam et sanguinem, sicut Ioannes scripsit, ut aqua tingueretur sanguine glorificaretur."

33. 16.2: "qui lavacrum et non acceptum repraesentat et perditum reddit."

34. 15.3: "Felix aqua semel abluit, quae ludibrio peccatoribus non est, quae non adsiduitate sordium infecta rursus quos diluit inquinat."

35. 18.4: "Itaque pro cuiusque personae condicione ac dispositione, etiam aetate, cunctatio baptismi utilior est praecipue, tamen circa parvulos."

36. Many Christians remained catechumens for most of their life, hoping to be baptized before they died. Emperor Constantine is the most famous case, but this practice was not uncommon. As late as 420 Augustine is on record as encouraging one Firmus to accept baptism and its responsibilities: *Ep.* 24.1–7, 7.4.

a holiday-time for sinning, rather than a time for learning not to sin."[37] So, while warning people not to rush into baptism, Tertullian also warns against using its postponement as an excuse not to start living a committed Christian life.

In conclusion, Tertullian laid the foundation for much of North Africa's teaching on the church as it relates both to the sacrament of baptism in water and to martyrdom, the baptism in blood. In the next two chapters, we shall examine how this tradition continued and how it was modified as Christians encountered other challenges, especially the first empire-wide persecution of the church.

---

37. *Paen.* 6.3: "Certi enim indubitatae veniae delictorum medium tempus interim furantur et commeatum sibi faciunt delinquendi quam eruditionem non delinquendi."

4

Cyprian on Persecution and Martyrdom

CYPRIAN, THE MAN

THANKS TO CYPRIAN'S EIGHTY or so letters and several treatises written during his episcopate (circa 248–258), we have a wealth of information about the circumstances and events surrounding his life as bishop of Carthage. On the other hand, we have no information concerning his tribal lineage, birthplace, or pre-conversion years. We can assume that he came from a family of some means, as he sold his inheritance to feed the poor.[1] And from his letters we can see that he was a man with a solid education. The account of his trial and martyrdom gives his name as both Thascius and Cyprianus;[2] According to Jerome, he took the name Caecilianus from the older bishop who led him to Christ.[3] Thus, he is also referred to as Thascius Caecilianus Cyprianus.

His biographer, the deacon Pontius, begins the narrative of Cyprian's life at Cyprian's baptism, informing us that the future martyr's talent and popularity caused him to move quickly up the ranks of the church. Within two years of his baptism, Cyprian was ordained a presbyter and shortly after that he was proclaimed bishop of Carthage by popular demand.[4] When Cyprian attempted to refuse this honor, public demonstrations were made, and Cyprian submitted to the pressure. Pontius emphasizes Cyprian's modesty and his charity toward the poor:

> His house was open to every comer. No widow returned from him
> with an empty lap; no blind man was unguided by him as a com-

1. Pontius, "Life" (ANF 5:267).
2. Murrillo, *Acts,* 11: "Tu es Thascius qui et Cyprianus."
3. Jerome, *Vir. ill.* 3.
4. Pontius, "Life" (ANF 5:269).

panion; none faltering in step was unsupported by him for a staff; none stripped of help by the hand of the mighty was not protected by him as a defender.[5]

That the people should insist on a man of such character becoming their bishop comes as no surprise. Pontius reports, however, that some of the older presbyters resented this novice's swift elevation to the office of bishop. Perhaps Cyprian's biographer thought it necessary to mention this resentment to explain the harsh opposition and division that surfaced after the Decian persecution; but Pontius goes on to say that Cyprian's patience and kindness won over those who had resented his election.[6] Nevertheless, a remnant of dissident clergy, deacons, and confessors later challenged his authority when the church in North Africa was most vulnerable, so that the newly elected bishop needed both his rhetorical and writing skills and his popularity among the laity to hold the church together.

Shortly after his election, possibly in 248, the novice bishop had to face the most intense persecution of the church to date. When he fled to protect his life and calm the situation, some of the clergy who resented his election used his flight to discredit his ministry and challenge his authority. Nonetheless, Cyprian was able to hold his church together by encouraging its office holders to remain faithful. Let us look at the various offices and ministries Bishop Cyprian had at his disposal.

THE NORTH AFRICAN CHURCH: ITS OFFICES AND MINISTRIES

Cyprian's letters give us a wealth of knowledge concerning the ordained offices and ministries in the church at Carthage. At the top is the office of the bishop, who was the pastor and leader of the church in his diocese. The diocese was understood to be one church under the bishop as pastor, but by Cyprian's time a diocese could have several local churches over which the bishop acted as leader. Cyprian, however, as the bishop of the metropolitan city of Carthage, exercised influence beyond his diocese over the churches throughout North Africa. Other bishops respected

---

5. Pontius, *Vita Cypriani* 3: "Domus eius patuit cuicumque venienti: nulla vidua revocata sinu vacuo, nullus indigens lumine non illo comite directus est, nullus debilis gressu non illo baiulo vectus est, nullus nudus auxilio de potentioris manu non illo tutore protectus est."

6. Pontius, *Vita Cypriani* 5.

the bishops of large cities like Carthage and Rome and often sought their advice. As J. Patout Burns notes: "As bishop of the provincial capital and chief city of Roman Africa, the bishop of Carthage summoned and presided over synods of his fellow bishops which formulated common policy and exercised discipline over the bishops themselves."[7] In exercising this discipline, Cyprian and other bishops could excommunicate recalcitrant bishops and decide the proper penance for fallen Christians.

In Africa and in Rome the bishops were elected by other leaders in the local church or by neighboring churches with the consent of the community. Cyprian's popularity among the people decided his election as bishop.[8]

Celibacy was not demanded of bishops and priests in the Western church until long after Cyprian's time. Cyprian may have had a wife, but the interpretation of Pontius' Latin text on this point has been challenged.[9] Nothing in Cyprian's writings, however, suggests that he opposed married clergy, and his mentor Caecilius, who is credited with winning him to Christ, was a married priest.[10]

Below the bishop was the office of the priest or presbyter. The priests assisted the bishop, and from this group a bishop was usually chosen. From Cyprian's letters we know that they not only received a stipend for themselves but also collected church money that they were responsible for distributing to various ministries outside the walls of the church.[11] Moreover, some priests were designated by Cyprian as teacher-presbyters, responsible for examining with the bishop which readers (holders of a lower clerical office) were qualified to teach the "hearers," those preparing for clerical office.[12]

7. Burns, *Cyprian*, 15.

8. Pontius, *Vita Cypriani* 5.

9. Pontius, *Vita Cypriani* 3. The ANF translation states: "Neither poverty nor pain broke him down; the persuasion of his wife did not influence him;" On the other hand, other scholars believe Cyprian did not have a wife and that the text in Pontius, 3 (*non uxoris suadela deflexit*) was misinterpeted. Cyprian, *Letters* (tr. Clarke), 1:127. Whatever the correct interpretation of this text, it would not be unusual for a wealthy Carthaginian to be married before entering the church.

10. Pontius, *Vita Cypriani* 4. According to Pontius, Cyprian agreed to care for Caecilius' wife and children after his death. Cyprian's acceptance of such a charge makes more sense if he was married than if he was single.

11. Cyprian, *Ep.* 5.1. Concering stipends, see *Ep.* 41.1.

12. Cyprian, *Ep.* 29.

Close in rank to the presbyters or priests were the deacons. Cyprian in hiding addressed most of his letters to the presbyters and deacons, asking them to carry out his duties as well as their own. For example, in several of his letters Cyprian admonishes them to feed the poor and to care for widows, strangers, and the confessors in prison.[13] Cyprian also instructs them to record the date of each martyr's death so that the church could properly celebrate the martyrs' memorials.[14]

Occasionally, Cyprian mentions the offices of sub-deacon and acolyte. It appears that the acolyte assisted the sub-deacon in carrying out the bishop's wishes. Cyprian used his sub-deacons and acolytes to transport his letters to other parts of the empire and to bring back letters written to him by other bishops.[15]

Lastly, Cyprian mentions in several letters the office of lector or reader. In connection with this office Cyprian reveals an important facet of his thinking on ordination. When Cyprian informs the Roman church of the ordination of Celerinus and Aurelius to the office of lector, he insists that what they suffered as confessors has already ordained them to an office in the church; as bishop, he simply had the job of placing them in the appropriate office:[16]

> Let the voice that has confessed the Lord daily be heard in those things which the Lord spoke. Let it be seen whether there is any further degree to which he can be advanced in the Church. There is nothing in which a confessor can do more good to the brethren than that while the reading of the Gospel is heard from his lips, every one who hears should imitate the faith of the reader.[17]

13. Cyprian, *Ep.* 7. In this letter, Cyprian tells his leaders that they can take from his money to help feed those in need, if necessary. In *Ep.* 62 Cyprian reports that he allocated 100,000 sesterces as a ransom payment to release captured Christians from Numidia.

14. Cyprian, *Ep.* 12.1. Cyprian also insists that Christians who died in prison before they were tortured were to be considered martrys.

15. Cyprian, *Ep.* 14.4.

16. Cyprian, *Ep.* 38.2: "Such a one to be estimated not by his years but by his deserts, merited higher degrees of clerical ordination and larger increase. But, in the meantime, I judged it well that he should begin with the office of reading." The translation used here is from ANF.

17. Cyprian, *Ep.* 39 .1-2: "Vox dominum confessa in his cotidie quae dominus locutus est audiatur. Viderit an sit ulterior gradus ad quem profici in ecclesia possit. Nihil est in quo magis confessor fratribus prosit quam ut, dum evangelica lectio de ore eius auditur, lectoris fidem quisque audierit imitetur."

In accord with this thinking, Cyprian bypassed the usual custom of meeting with other church leaders to discuss the candidates' fitness for ordination, since he believed that the confessors had already been evaluated by God through their suffering.[18]

In summary, Cyprian's letters mention the following ministerial offices: bishop, presbyter/priest, deacon, sub-deacon, lector, and acolyte.[19]

WHERE IS THE CHURCH AFTER MARTYRDOM?

Cyprian developed further the North African thinking on the relationship of martyrdom (the baptism in blood) to the sacrament of baptism and to membership in the church. In chapters two and three we noticed how persecution led many Christians to choose martyrdom over denial of Christ. Tertullian insisted, in defiance of the Roman authorities, that the blood of the martyrs caused the church to grow.[20]

During the middle of the third century, however, the church in Rome and North Africa developed a new understanding of the traditional theology of martyrdom and water baptism as previously discussed by Tertullian. During the Decian persecution (249–251) martyrdom influenced the Church in both positive and negative ways. For example, the confessors' traditional power of pardon now was seen to challenge the authority of the local bishop. Confessors (soon to be martyrs) pardoned persons for various sins and admitted them back into the church before they had completed their penance and received the blessing of their bishop. Rigorist Christians in Rome and North Africa then challenged the more lenient Christians in those areas by refusing to admit these lapsed persons back into the Church. Thus, the Decian persecution cast older traditions concerning penance in a new light and added new problems. As a result, the bishops of Rome, Asia and North Africa were forced to reexamine issues related to the very nature of the church. They were forced to examine the question: "Where is the church?"

18. Cyprian, *Ep.*38.1: "But human testimonies must not be waited for when the divine approval precedes. Aurelius, our brother, an illustrious youth, already approved by the Lord."

19. Burns, *Cyprian*, 16. Burns points out that each of these offices had age requirements, specific duties, and assigned compensation. The church at Carthage was well organized.

20. Tertullian, *Apol.* 50.

To understand the Africans' concept of what constituted a church, we must follow the development of the theology of the sacrament of water baptism and the baptism in blood in North African ecclesiology. We will then be able to appreciate the distinct traditions that developed in North Africa and Rome.

This was not a new question; it had been addressed in various ways since the beginning of Christianity. Often misunderstood and on the defensive, early Christian leaders such as Irenaeus and Tertullian developed Christian doctrine in an attempt to exclude various heretical groups and guide believers to what they considered the proper teachings of the church. The apostles' creed, the rule of faith, and the concept of apostolic succession attempted to define both the authentic Christian tradition and the constitution of the church. The leaders of the early church developed a sense of tradition as they defended their understanding of scripture against Marcion and others whom they deemed heretics. It was in this context that the early church developed the rule of faith based upon apostolic preaching, as Georges Florovsky points out:

> When Christians spoke of the "Rule of Faith" as "Apostolic," they did not mean that the Apostles had met and formulated it. . . . What they meant was that the profession of belief which every catechumen recited before his baptism did embody in summary form the faith which the Apostles had taught and committed to their disciples to teach after them.[21]

The definition of the rule of faith had consequences for ecclesiology: North African and Roman Christians agreed that the church exists where the proper teaching, as defined by the rule of faith, is present and where the sacraments are administered through a properly ordained priest or bishop.[22] Consequently, both groups agreed that one entered the church through the sacrament of baptism, at which time the new Christian recited and affirmed the rule of faith.[23] The Decian persecution, however,

21. Florovsky, *Tradition*, 76.

22. The offices of bishop, presbyter, and deacon became important early in the development of the church. Ignatius, *Tral.* 1.3: "Similiarly, let everyone respect the deacons as Jesus Christ, just as they should respect the bishop, who is the model of the Father, and the presbyters as God's council and as the band of the apostles. Without these no group can be called a church." Translation from Lightfoot, *Fathers*, 98.

23. The second-century document entitled *The Shepherd of Hermes* states: "The seal, therefore, is the water, so they go down in the water dead and they come up alive. Thus

gave rise to conflict between the Roman and North African churches concerning the proper boundaries of the church.

DECIUS' RISE TO POWER AND THE OUTBREAK OF PERSECUTION

Since its inception, Christianity had suffered persecutions at various times and places throughout the empire. These persecutions, however severe, involved few persons and were usually sporadic and always local.[24] However, between 249 and 251, individual Christians as well as the church as an institution encountered their severest test up to that point when the emperor Decius instituted the first empire-wide persecution. Various external factors apparently led Decius to decide on this attack against the church. The Goths were intruding into Roman territory, and Emperor Philip turned to C. Messius Quintus Decius, the perfect of the city of Rome, to defeat them. Decius succeeded, temporarily driving the Goths back across the Danube. This success inspired his troops to declare him emperor against his wishes, leading to a showdown between him and Philip. After several months of unsuccessful negotiations, Decius defeated Philip at Verona.[25] Shortly after becoming emperor in 249, Decius, desiring, in the words of Burns, "to consolidate his position as well as to secure the good fortune of his reign, decreed that every citizen should join him in offering homage to the immortal gods, whose graciousness secured the peace and prosperity of the empire."[26] Decius took for himself the name of Trajan, one of Rome's greatest emperors; and in emulation of his namesake he attempted, on the occasion of Rome's first millennium, to bring the empire together by reawakening loyalty to the gods that had made the city great. Although Decius' edict has not survived, we know from Cyprian's writings that Christians were ordered to pour a libation, offer incense, and eat the sacrificial meats.[27] Those doing so were granted a certificate (*libellus*) attesting to their compliance. From an analysis of

---

the seal was proclaimed to them as well and they may use it in order that they might enter the kingdom of God." Translation from Lightfoot, *Fathers*, 498–9. See also Tertullian, *Bapt.* 1.1.

24. Evans, *One and Holy*, 36.

25. Frend, *Rise*, 318–19.

26. Burns, *Cyprian*, 1.

27. Cyprian, *Laps.* 8, 9, 14, 20, 25, 27, 28, 34.

the surviving *libelli*, Allen Brent maintains that Decius intended to build upon the extension of citizenship by Emperor Caracalla in 212 to all inhabitants of the empire.[28] Decius held that this citizenship entailed the obligation to respect Rome's traditional gods, thus appeasing their possible anger at a time of peril for the empire.

Cyprian pointedly describes Decius' reaction to Christian refusal to conform to traditional religious practices: "News that a rival emperor was being raised up against him [Decius] would receive with far greater patience and forbearance than word that a bishop of God was being appointed in Rome."[29] Accordingly, Decius first attacked the leadership of the church. From December 249 to February 250, bishops were sought out and arrested. Fabian, bishop of Rome, and Babylas, bishop of Antioch, were arrested and executed; bishop Alexander of Jerusalem died in prison; Cyprian went into hiding.[30] From exile Cyprian attempted to govern his church by letter, but power struggles arose in both North Africa and Rome, and the church in most of the empire was thrown into disarray. And then, in a second phase of the persecution, Decius began to enforce on all citizens the demand to sacrifice to the Roman gods, aiming to force Christians either to comply with the law or to suffer imprisonment and possible execution.[31] The church had indeed grown in numbers by this time, but most of its members were not ready to receive a baptism in blood.

MARTYRDOM AND THE DECIAN PERSECUTION

From 249 to around 258, martyrdom was a real possibility for any Christian living within the Roman Empire. Several sporadic attacks followed Decius' first empire-wide persecution. Emperor Gallus started the persecution again, though not in Africa. When Emperor Valerian launched a persecution in 257–9, both Stephen of Rome and Cyprian were martyred. Thus, the threat of persecution hung over Cyprian's entire episcopate. In his desire to hold a wounded church together, Cyprian sent

28. Brent, *Cyprian*, 178.

29. Cyprian, *Ep.* 55.9: "Eo tempore cum tyrannus infestus sacerdotibus dei fanda comminaretur, cum multo patientius et tolerabilius audiret levari avuersus se aemulum principem quam constitui Romae dei sacerdotem."

30. Frend, *Rise*, 319.

31. Frend, *Martyrdom*, 407.

out letter after letter instructing some, admonishing others, and encouraging all who would listen. Early in the Decian persecution, in what may have been one of his first letters to his deacons and presbyters, Cyprian writes:

> I send greeting to you, my dearest brothers, safe as I am by the grace of God, and I rejoice to learn that for your part you, too, are completely safe. The circumstances of my present position do not allow me to be there with you at the moment; and I, therefore, ask of you, in accordance with your faith and devotion, to discharge in Carthage not only your duties but mine as well, ensuring hereby that discipline and zeal are fully maintained.[32]

Cyprian here wrote with a certain calm as he instructed his deacons to carry out not only their duties but his as well; the persecution is apparently not yet severe and there are no reports of martyrs. However, within a month or so of this letter the Decian persecution had intensified: martyrdoms are reported. Cyprian's letters from this point on take on a more urgent tone. Like Tertullian before him, Cyprian draws upon the imagery of a soldier in battle, exhorting:

> The combat has increased, and with that the glory of the combatants. You have not hung back from the battlefront from fear of the tortures; rather the tortures have themselves incited you on to join the battlefront. Courageous, steadfast, you have advanced with generous self-sacrifice into the very heart of the fighting. Some of your number, I hear, have already received their crowns; others are very close to winning their crowns of victory.[33]

Although Cyprian knows that Christians had been both tortured and martyred, it appears that they had met the challenge. In fact, in the same letter Cyprian singles out the recent martyr, Mappalicus, as an example for other Christians to follow:

32. Cyprian, *Ep.* 5.1: "Saluto vos incolumis per Dei gratiam, fratres carissimi, laetus quod circa incolumitatem quoque vestram omnia integra esse cognoverim. Et quoniam mihi interesse nunc non permittit lici condicio, peto vos pro fide et religione vestra fungamini illic et vestris partibus et meis, ut nihil vel ad disciplinam vel ad diligentiam desit." Epistles 5, 6, 7, 13, and 14 were written while Cyprian was in hiding but do not refer to any martyrs; thus, they are considered his earliest espistles.

33. Cyprian, *Ep.*10.1–2: "Crevit pugna, crevit et pugnantium gloria. Nec retardati estis ab acie tormentorum metu, sed ipsis tormentis magis estis ad aciem provocati, fortes et stabiles ad maximi certaminis proelium prompta devotione prodistis. Ex quibus quosdam iam conperi coronatos, quosdam vero ad coronam victoriae proximos."

> My prayer and my exhortation is that the rest of you follow him,
> now a most blessed martyr, and the others, who were his partners
> in the same conflict and his companions, who proved themselves
> in faith steadfast, in pain long-suffering, in interrogation victo-
> rious. May those who have been united by lodging together in
> prison and by the bond of confession be thus united also in the
> culmination of their heavenly crowns.[34]

In another letter written around the same time, Cyprian admonishes the
presbyters and deacons to honor even those who have died in prison before their blood baptism:

> You should pay special care and solicitude also to the bodies of
> all those who, without being tortured, nevertheless die in prison,
> departing this life in glory. They are inferior neither in valor nor
> in honor so that they, too, should be added to the company of the
> blessed martyrs. They have endured, in so far as they were able,
> whatever they were prepared and ready to endure. A man who
> under the eyes of God has offered himself to torture and to death
> has in fact suffered whatever he was willing to suffer, He did not
> fail the tortures, they failed him.[35]

During these times of persecution martyrs were held up to the community as the example of the perfect witness, for the true martyr or confessor refused to deny Christ no matter what the cost. No person could
receive this gift unless God gave it.[36] In fact, Cyprian encourages the
Christians of Thibaris by reminding them that all men and women must
die some day; the current persecution could be viewed as an opportunity
to do what we all must do, but with the privilege of receiving a crown in
the process.

---

34. Cyprian, *Ep.* 10.4: "Istum nunc beatissimum martyrem et alios participes eius-
dem congressionis et comites in fide stabiles, in dolore patientes, in quaestione victores
ut ceteri quoque sectemini et opto pariter et exhortor, ut quos vinculum confessionis et
hospitium carceris simul iunxit iungat etiam consummatio virtutis et corona caelestis."

35. Cyprian, *Ep.* 12.1–2: "Corporibus etiam omnium, qui etsi torti non sunt, in
carcere tamem florioso exitu mortis excedunt, inpertiatur et vigilantia et cura propen-
sior. Neque enim virtus eorum aut honor minor est quominus ipsi quoque inter beatos
martyras adgregentur. Quod in illis est toleraverunt quidquid tolerare parati et prompti
fuerunt. Qui se tormentis et morti sub oculis Dei obtulit passus est quidquid pati voluit.
Non enim ipse tormentis, sed tormenta ipsi defuerunt."

36. Tertullian and Cyprian agreed that martyrdom was a gift from God: Tertullian,
Mart. 1.3, Cyprian, *De Mortalitate*, 17.

Cyprian's words of encouragement to the confessors were not without results. When bishop Fabian of Rome had succumbed to martyrdom, Cyprian continued to correspond with the deacons and presbyters in the holy city. After several months of silence, Cyprian finally received a response from them, stating that they agreed with his position requiring the lapsed to complete their prescribed penance before returning to the church and informing him that his words in the absence of their bishop had not only blessed them but had also encouraged some to make the ultimate sacrifice:

> And at this point it is our duty to pay you a duty we happily render, the greatest and most abundant of thanks. By your letter the darkness of their prison you have filled with light; you have visited them by the way through which you could gain entry; their hearts, stalwart in their faith and in their confession, you have refreshed by the comforting words of your letter; their triumphs you have lauded with fitting praises and you have thus enflamed them with even more ardent yearning for heavenly glory; you have driven onwards men already straining at the task; by the strength of your exhortation you have given fresh heart to those who we believe and pray will one day be victorious. It is true that all of this may seem to depend on the faith of those who confess and on the favor of God; nevertheless, as a result of your letter, they would seem to have become in some measures your debtors in their martyrdom.[37]

In hiding or not, Cyprian never ceased to encourage those faced with the challenge of martyrdom to stand firm. And when the time came for his test, he withdrew for a while, but only to allow himself to be martyred in the city in which he served as bishop.[38] For Cyprian believed that a bishop should confess and be martyred among his flock: "It is fit for a bishop, in that city in which he presides over the church of the Lord, there to confess the Lord, and that the whole people should be glorified by the confession of their prelate in their presence. For whatever in that mo-

---

37. Cyprian, *Ep.* 30.5–1: "In quo loco maximas tibi atque uberes gratias referre debemus et reddimus quod illorum carceris tenebras litteris tuis inluminasti, quod ad illos venisti quomodo introire potuisti, quod illorum animos sua fide et confessione robustos tuis adlocutionibus litterisque recreasti, quod felicitates eorum condignis laudibus prosecutus accendisti ad multo ardentiorem caelestis gloriae cupiditatem, quod pronos inpulisti quod ut credimus et optamus victores futuros viribus tui sermonis animasti, ut quamquam hoc totum de fide confitentium et de divina indulgentia venire videatur, tamen in martyrio suo tibi ex aliquo debitores facti esse videantur."

38. Musurillo, *Acts,* 171.

ment of confession the confessor-bishop speaks, he speaks in the mouth of all, by inspiration of God."[39] And what inspired words did Cyprian confess before all at his execution? The words of the Scillitan Martyrs, *Deo gratias* ("thanks be to God"), a phrase that was to become famous among African Christians. Cyprian's steadfast faith and his ability to back up his faith with action made him a hero in North Africa for generations to come.[40] Moreover, his martyrdom gave credence to his claim that he fled during the Decian persecution not out of fear but for the sake of his flock, until the time appointed for his martyrdom. That he was the first African bishop to receive the baptism in blood influenced future generations of African Christians to take pride in calling themselves the church of the martyrs. For to be in the church of the martyrs was to identify with their greatest hero, Saint Cyprian. In this way, martyrdom, the baptism in blood, would continue to give the church in Africa a sense of pride.[41]

Nonetheless, during Cyprian's own lifetime the confessors and martyrs also wrought havoc in the Church. Although many Christians received crowns of martyrdom and many others withstood tortures, most of the Christians confronted with a baptism in blood were not prepared to receive it; they either sacrificed to the Roman gods or purchased a false certificate stating that they had done so. When the Decian persecution ended, many of these fallen Christians wanted to be readmitted to the church. Because opinions varied, there was a crisis throughout the church concerning the proper response to this demand. Jane Merdinger captures the dilemma:

> In the months following the cessation of persecution, numbers of
> Christians repented of their folly and began to seek readmission to
> the church. What were bishops to do? Should they deny penitents
> reentry to the church, given the gravity of the sin of apostasy, or

39. Cyprian, *Ep.* 81.1–2: "Congruit episcopum in ea civitate in qua ecclesiae dominicae praeest illic dominum confiteri et plebem universam praepositi praesentis confessione clarificari. Quidcumque enim sub ipso confessionis momento confessor episcopus loquitur aspirante deo ore omnium loquitur."

40. Musurillo, *Acts*, 172.

41. Pontius in *Vita Cypriani* 19 (ANF 5:274) writes, "His passion being thus accomplished, it resulted that Cyprian, who had been an example to all good men, was also the first who in Africa imbued his priestly crown with blood of martyrdom, because he was the first who began to be such after the apostles."

should they relax traditional demands in light of the overwhelming numbers of the lapsed?[42]

Throughout the Decian persecution, Cyprian had corresponded with several clergy and lay persons discussing what should be done in these cases. Traditionally, lapsed persons were not allowed back into the church; however, the general consensus held that no final decision should be made concerning the lapsed until the church was at peace and could meet in council to decide the matter.[43] In the meantime, Cyprian and the Roman presbyters insisted that lapsed persons should continue performing their penance in an effort to appease the God whom they had so recently offended.

The majority of Christians seemed to agree with this decision. In Carthage, however, the presbyter Fortunatus, in opposition to bishop Cyprian, began to readmit lapsed persons back into the church on the premise that they had received permission from the martyrs or confessors to return.[44] This not only added more confusion to the already divided church but also pitted the highly esteemed martyrs and confessors against their local bishop. The deacon Felicissimus, on the other hand, refused to receive back into the church anyone who had committed apostasy, either through sacrifice or through the purchase of a *libellus*.[45] Thus, by the time Cyprian finally returned to Carthage from hiding he was faced with the challenge of bringing both healing and unity to a severely wounded and divided church.

At the same time, Rome was experiencing similar problems. In an attempt to challenge the reigning bishop Cornelius who held a relatively lenient position concerning the lapsed, Novatian had himself elected bishop in opposition to Cornelius; and when he was unsuccessful in unseating Cornelius, he started rival churches in Rome and Carthage that denied any admittance to the lapsed.[46]

Thus, at the conclusion of the Decian persecution the church was faced with at least three factions: 1) rigorists in both Rome and Carthage who refused any mercy to the lapsed; 2) a more lenient group that used

42. Merdinger, *Rome*, 37.

43. Cyprian calls for such a council in *Ep.* 20, 26, 33, 34, 55, and 57.

44. Cyprian, *Ep.* 59.

45. Cyprian, *Ep.* 43.

46. Cyprian, *Ep.* 44 and 55.

confessors and martyrs to admit lapsed persons back into the church before they had completed the penance prescribed by their bishops and,
indeed, in some cases before they had done any penance at all;[47] and 3)
Cyprian and other moderate leaders who asked for patience and submis-
sion to clerical authority until the persecution ended, at which time the
church could meet in council to settle the matter. These challenges forced
church leaders to rethink the question: "Where is the church?" Cyprian
wrote two major works, *De Lapsis* and *De Unitate*, attempting to answer
this question.

WHERE IS THE CHURCH?

In his work *De lapsis* (*On the Lapsed*), Cyprian faced the challenge of
showing respect for the confessors and martyrs on the one hand while
upholding the authority of the bishop on the other. He begins by honor-
ing the confessors:

> Our confessors are a joy to look upon, men whose renown is on
> every tongue, whose courage and faith have covered them with
> glory; long have we yearned after them with passionate longing,
> and we embrace them at last, and affectionately impress on them
> the sacred kiss. They form the bright army of soldiers of Christ,
> whose steadfastness broke the fierce onslaught of persecution,
> ready as they were for the long-suffering of prison life, steeled to
> the endurance of death. Valiantly you resisted the world's attack; to
> God you offered a glorious spectacle, to your brethren an example
> to follow.[48]

Cyprian continued his praise of the confessors, being careful to acknowledge the women and the youth alike:

> With joy in her breast does Mother Church receive you back
> from the fray! How blessed, how happy she is to open her gates
> for you to enter as in closed ranks, you bear the trophies of the

47. Cyprian, *Ep.* 22 and 53.

48. *Laps.* 2: "Confessores praeconio boni nominis claros et virtutis ac fidei laudibus
gloriosos laetis conspectibus intuemur; sanctis osculis adhaerentes desideratos diu in-
explebili cupiditate conplectimur. Adest militum Christi cohors candida, qui persecutionis urgentis ferociam turbulentam stabili congressione fregerunt, parati ad patientiam
carceris, armati ad tolerantiam mortis. Repugnastis fortiter saeculo, spectaculum glorio-
sum praebuistis Deo, secuturis fratibus fuistis exemplo." The translation of *De lapsis* and
De ecclesae catholicae unitate here given is by Maurice Bèvenot, S.J.

vanquished foe! Joining the victory of their men, come the women too, triumphing over the world and over their sex alike. With them also, celebrating a double victory, come the virgins and boys with virtues beyond their years.[49]

Cyprian closes this first section of the treatise by expressing his sorrow at the abuse and mistreatment the confessors and martyrs had suffered:

These heavenly crowns of the martyrs, these spiritual triumphs of the confessors, these outstanding exploits of our brethren cannot, alas, remove one cause of sorrow: that the enemy's violence and slaughter have wrought havoc amongst us and have torn away something from our very heart and cast it to the ground. What shall I do, dear brethren, in face of this? My mind tosses this way and that. What shall I say? How shall I say it? Tears and not words alone express the grief which so deep a wound in our body calls for, which the great gaps in our once numerous flock evoke from our hearts. Who could be so callous, so stony-hearted, who so un-mindful of brotherly love, as to remain dry-eyed in the presence of so many of his own kin who are broken now, shadows of their former selves.[50]

Thus Cyprian, as a loving pastor, was careful to speak in glowing terms of the martyrs and confessors before he turned to disagree with them; he did not want to be seen as disrespectful to such a distinguished group. Nevertheless, as the bishop of a church reduced in size and wound-ed, he had to warn the remnant that this dark and cruel persecution could not be allowed to blind Christians from doing what God was now urg-

---

49. *Laps.* 2: "Quam vos laeto sinu excipit mater ecclesia de proelio revertentes. Quam beata, quam gaudens portas suas aperit, ut adunatis agminibus intretis de hoste pros-trato tropaea referentes. Cum triumphantibus viris et feminae veniunt quae cum saeculo sexum quoque vicerunt. Veniunt et geminata militiae suae gloria virgines et pueri annos suos virtutibus transeuntes."

50. *Laps.* 4: "Has martyrum caelestes coronas, has confessorum glorias spiritales, has stantium fratrum maximas eximiasque virtutes maestitia una contristat: quod avulsam nostrorum viscerum partem violentus inimicus populationis suae strage deiecit. Quid hoc loco faciam, dilectissimi fratres, fluctuans vario mentis aestu quid aut quomodo dicam.? Lacrimis magis quam verbis opus est ad exprimendum dolorem quo corporis nostri plaga deflenda est, quo populi aliquando numerosi multiplex lamentanda iactura est. Quis enim sic durus ac ferreus, quis sic fraternae caritatis oblitus qui, inter suorum multiformes ruinas et lugubres ac multo squalore deformes reliquias constitutus."

ing.[51] Cyprian likens himself to a responsible doctor who must cut out the infected part from his patient regardless of the pain; it is for the patient's own good, and in the end the patient will thank him. Cyprian insists that as bishop he must teach and speak the truth to the church, however painful, because doing so is for Christians' benefit. Thus, Cyprian can say that, though the acts of the confessors and martyrs should be respected, the confessors must obey the gospel; and in Cyprian's view, to admit lapsed persons back into the church before they have completed their penance is contrary to the gospel. Thus, after praising the confessors and martyrs, he must now challenge them to obey the gospel:

> For, dear brethren, there has now appeared a new source of disaster and, as if the fierce storm of persecution had not been enough, there has come to crown it a subtle evil, an innocent seeming pestilence, which masquerades as compassion. Contrary to the full strength of the gospel, contrary to the law of our Lord and God, through certain people's presumption a deceptive readmission to communion is being granted, a reconciliation that is null and void, one that imperils givers and is worthless to those who receive it.[52]

Cyprian denounced the innovation allowing persons back into the church without completing their penance. He insists that the lapsed should seek the slow, painful road to recovery requiring constant prayer for God's forgiveness until their penance is complete and the remorseful sinners can have hands laid upon them and be readmitted to the eucharist:

> You must beg and pray assiduously, spend the day sorrowing and the night in vigils and tears, fill every moment with weeping and lamentation; you must lie on the ground amidst clinging ashes, toss about chaffing in sackcloth and foulness; having once been clothed with Christ, refuse all other raiment now; having supped with the devil, choose rather now to fast; apply yourself to good deeds which can wash away your sins, be constant and generous in giving alms, whereby souls are freed from death.[53]

51. *Laps.* 5.

52. *Laps.* 15: "Emersit enim, fratres dilectissimi, novum genus cladis et quasi parum persecutionis procella saevierit, accessit ad cumulum sub misericordiae titulo malum fallens et blanda pernicies. Contra evangelii vigorem, contra Domini ac Dei legem temeritate quorundam laxatur incautis communicatio: inrita et falsa pax, periculosa dantibus et nihil accipientibus profutura."

53. *Laps.* 34: "Orare oportet inpensius et rogare; diem luctu transigere, vigiliis noctes ac fletibus ducere, tempus omne lacrimosis lamentationibus occupare; stratos solo ad-

The road back for the lapsed was hard, but to be deceived into not doing the required penance was not only a tragedy but in Cyprian's view a new type of persecution, even worse than the Decian persecution itself. For this false reconciliation did as much harm to the lapsed as hail does to crops or as a wild tempest does to trees;[54] the lapsed who accept such a compromise are headed for destruction because they are not following the gospel. True Christians must put their faith in the gospel, not in the confessors:

> If those who deny Him are not held guilty of a crime, neither shall those who confess Him receive the reward of virtue. But if the victory of faith receives its crown, defeat through lack of faith must receive its punishment. Therefore, either the martyrs avail nothing, if the gospel fails, or, if the gospel cannot fail, then those whom the gospel enables to become martyrs, cannot act in opposition to the gospel.[55]

After these stern words, Cyprian reminds his readers that although no one should try to rob the martyrs of their glory and crown, "those themselves who have fulfilled the commands of God cannot instigate the bishops to act against the command of God."[56] One cannot assume that the prayers of the martyrs will automatically win favor with God; only petitions in accord with God's word and God's desire will receive a positive answer. Cyprian cites several outstanding biblical figures (Moses, Ezekiel, and Jeremiah) who prayed to God without response because their petitions did not accord with God's will. Cyprian points out that only God can forgive sins and that sins "committed against Him can be canceled by Him alone who bore our sins and suffered for us."[57] This is, of course, a commonplace of Christian teaching, but Cyprian uses it here to challenge

---

haerere cineri, in cilicio et sordibus volutari; post indumentum Christi perditum, nullum iam velle vestitum, post diaboli cibum malle ieiunium; iustis operibus incumbere quibus peccata purgantur, elemosynis frequenter insistere quibus a morte animae liberantur."

54. *Laps.* 20.

55. *Laps.* 20: "Si negantes rei criminis non erunt, nec confitentes praemium virtutis accipiunt; porro si fides quae vicerit coronatur, necesse est et victa perfidia puniatur. Ita martyres aut nihil possunt si evangelium facere non possunt qui de evangelio martyres fiunt."

56. *Laps.* 20: "Ut ab episcopis contra mandatum Dei fiat, auctores esse non possunt qui ipsi Dei mandata fecerunt."

57. *Laps.* 17: "Veniam peccatis quae in ipsum commissa sunt solus potest ille largiri qui peccata nostra portavit."

the authority of the confessors who had not only usurped the authority of the bishop but had even infringed upon the authority of God;[58] for when a lapsed sinner went to a confessor for relief, sought the confessor's prayers for forgiveness and readmittance to the Church, the sinner in effect gave the confessor the honor and power due to God alone. As discussed in chapter two, Tertullian would not grant to any person, not even a bishop, the power to forgive grave sins such as adultery, murder and apostasy; only a baptism in blood could wash such sins away. Cyprian more leniently holds out the possibility of forgiveness even of such sins—but only at the hands of a bishop, not those of a confessor, because the bishop administers church discipline according to the gospel and under the direction of the Holy Spirit.

For Cyprian, therefore, the question "Where is the church?" can be answered without reservation: the church is where the bishop is present, given to the church to guide and direct it. Confessors and martyrs are worthy to receive honor and respect, but their authority is subject to the guidance of their bishop.

58. *Laps.* 17.

5

Cyprian and the Unity of the Church

DEVELOPMENTS IN THE CHURCH of his time, particularly around the Decian persecution, forced Cyprian to deal extensively with the question of church unity, and in the course of dealing with this issue a serious rift on ecclesiology developed between the North African and Roman churches. In his work *De lapsis* Cyprian argues forcefully that the bishops and not the martyrs and confessors have the authority and oversight over the church;[1] the church is where the bishop is present as Christ's representative. Moreover, as Christ's representative, the bishop can offer sacrifice (the eucharist) and petition God for satisfaction or forgiveness of sins on behalf of the sinner.[2] Cyprian also outlines the penalties that sinners should be subject to. However, shortly after this work, in late 251, Cyprian and other North African bishops met in council and made some adjustments to what Cyprian had outlined in *De lapsis*. Cyprian reports the outcome of this council in a letter to bishop Antonianus of Numidia.[3] The council agreed that mercy should be offered to fallen Christians so they would not get discouraged and return to the world (that is, abandon Christianity) or come under the influence of heretics or schismatics.[4] Concretely, the following decisions were made regarding the lapsed. First, it was decided that each case should be examined individually, with circumstances considered in determining the appropriate penance. Second, those who had purchased a certificate (*libellus*) stating they had sacrificed when in fact they had not should be readmitted to the church immediately if they had been faithful in doing their penance up to that point. Third, those who actually sacrificed to the idols were to continue their

1. *Laps.* 14.
2. *Laps.* 17.
3. *Ep.* 55.
4. *Ep.* 55.19.

penance for the remainder of their lives; they were assured, however, that they would be admitted to communion at the point of death and that if they became gravely ill while doing penance, they would also be admitted to communion immediately.[5] In defense of these changes, Cyprian said he wanted to balance God's justice with His mercy. Just as important, however, was his desire to maintain unity by preventing discouraged Christians from joining heretical or schismatic groups.

After the death of Decius in June 251, there was a break in the persecution of Christians; but churches throughout the empire were wounded not only from the scars of persecution but also from new divisions growing from within. In *De ecclesiae catholicae unitate* (*On the Unity of the Catholic Church*), often called simply *De unitate*, Cyprian concerns himself directly with unity in the church. He begins the work by reminding his "beloved brothers and sisters" that they are the "salt of the earth"[6] and as such they should be on guard to avoid the snares of the enemy, for Satan has invented heresies and schisms to sever the unity within the church. Though Cyprian does not name names, Merdinger maintains that the African bishop "is leveling his manifesto at specific troublesome targets—Felicissimus and Fortunatus of Carthage and Novatian of Rome."[7] However, Cyprian is certain that believers in Africa and Rome can avoid being deceived by these schismatics if they return to the source or origin of the church.

CYPRIAN AND THE CONCEPT OF *ORIGO*

Cyprian, like Tertullian before him, uses the concept of *origo* as a basis for the unity of the church, employing it, as did the earlier teacher, to address issues facing the church during his lifetime. Merdinger points out that "the fundamental concept underlying both Tertullian's and Cyprian's views of unity is that the source of a thing guarantees it essential unity."[8] The schisms of Novatian, Felicissimus or Fortunatus are deplorable to Cyprian because they try to introduce a second *origo* into the church. Cyprian counters this presumption by citing Christ's statement to Peter

5. *Ep.* 55.17.

6. *Unit. eccl.* 1: "Vos estis sal terrae."

7. Merdinger, *Rome*, 37–8. Epistles 55 and 59 show that Cyprian is speaking about these three men in *De unitate*.

8. Merdinger, *Rome*, 38–9.

that "upon this rock I will build my church"; Cyprian understands this to mean that Peter is the starting point or source (*origo*) on which the church is built.

In Cyprian's view, however, the power inherent in *origo* was given not to Peter alone but to all the apostles, and after them to every legitimate bishop proceeding from this source:

> The authority of the bishops forms a unity, of which each holds his part in its totality. And the church forms a unity, however far she spreads and multiplies by the progeny of her fecundity; just as the sun's rays are many, yet the light is one, and as a tree's branches are many, yet the strength deriving from its sturdy root is one. So too, when many streams are scattered abroad by the copiousness of the welling waters, yet their oneness abides by reason of their starting point.[9]

If the concept of *origo* was difficult for Cyprian's listeners to grasp in the abstract, his natural examples of the sun and its rays, tree branches and their root, and a stream flowing from a single source must have caught the imagination of his audience, living as it was in a largely agrarian society, and driven home his point: that there is only one source or origin in the church and that heretics and schismatics have sundered themselves from it and become rays separated from the sun, branches separated from their root, or streams dammed off from their source. In other words, one must at all costs stay connected to the unity of the church. Cyprian further insists that this unity is founded in the very Trinity of the Godhead:

> The Lord warns us when he says: "He that is not with me is against me, and he that gathers not with me, scatters." Whoever breaks the peace and harmony of Christ acts against Christ; whoever gathers elsewhere than in the church, scatters the church of Christ. The Lord says: "I and the Father are One"; and again, of Father, Son, and Holy Spirit it is written: "And the three are One." Does anyone think that this oneness, which derives from the stability of God and is welded together after the celestial pattern, can be sundered in the church and divided by the clash of discordant wills? If a man does not keep this unity, he is not keeping the law of God; he has

---

9. *Unit. eccl.* 5: "Episcopatus unus est cuius a singulis in solidum pars tenetur. Ecclesia una est quae in multitudinem latius incremento fecunditatis extenditur: quomodo solis multi radii sed lumen unum, et rami arboris multi sed robur unum tenaci radice fundatum, et cum de fonte uno rivi plurimi defluunt, numerositas licet diffusa videatur exundantis copiae largitate, unitas tamen servatur in origine."

broken faith with the Father and the Son, he is cut off from life and salvation.[10]

For Cyprian, to break the unity of the church by starting another church (which Cyprian calls a conventicle) is to separate oneself from the godhead and hence from salvation itself. Divisions caused by former bishops, now referred to as schismatics by Cyprian, are grave sins because the bishop must be one with the church. On this point, Evans captures the essence of Cyprian's teaching:

> When he speaks elsewhere of the "root," "origin," and "matrix" of the Church, it is not always clear whether he means the Catholic Church as such or the episcopate in particular, and indeed the distinction for him would be unreal, the one is unthinkable without the other; the constitution of the episcopate is the constituting of the church; the initial constitution of the episcopate in Peter sets forth the "origin" both of the episcopate and of the church.[11]

In light of this question we return to the question of the previous chapter: "Where is the church?" The church is where the properly ordained bishop is present. Peter Hinchliff summarizes this point: "If the church is in the bishop, as well as the bishop in the church, this is because the bishop is the focal point for the church's power as well as its life. The bishop ought always to act with his people."[12] If we appreciate Cyprian's view on the centrality of the bishop to the local church, then we can certainly understand why he was so harsh on leaders who he believed caused divisions in the church.

WHERE IS THE CHURCH AND WHO ARE ITS MEMBERS?

The divisions raging in the church forced Cyprian to grapple with this question also: "Who are the members of the church?" For after the

---

10. *Unit. eccl.* 6: "Monet Dominus et dicit: 'Qui non est mecum adversus me est, et qui non mecum colligit spargit.' Qui pacem Christi et concordiam rumpit, adversus Christum facit; qui alibi praeter ecclesiam colligit, Christi ecclesiam spargit. Dicit Dominus: 'Ego et Pater unm sumus', et iterum de Patre et Filio et Spiritu Sancto scriptum est: Et tres unum sunt. Et quisquam credit hanc unitatem de divina firmitate venientem, sacramentis caelestibus cohaerentem, scindi in ecclesia posse et voluntatum conlidentium divortio separari? Hanc unitatem qui non tenet non tenet Dei legem, non tenet Patris et Filii fidem, vitam non tenet et salutem."

11. Evans, *One and Holy*, 54.

12. Hinchliff, *Cyprian*, 104.

Decian persecution, this question became a point of fierce debate. On the one hand, Novatian and his followers taught that lapsed Christians should not be readmitted to the church.[13] In their view, such persons had forfeited their right to be Christians. Novatian also succeeded in having Maximus (one of his leaders) set up a rival church in Africa. As Burns correctly notes, Novatian "subsequently ordained and sent out bishops to establish faithful communities in cities where he judged the existing churches as having failed."[14] On the other hand, Cyprian showed mercy to lapsed Christians but excommunicated those schismatic bishops who opposed him in Africa, deeming Novatian and his followers to be outside the church. He also excommunicated five African presbyters, two of whom, Fortunatus and Felicissimus, went to Rome attempting to discredit Cyprian before Bishop Cornelius of Rome.[15] According to Cyprian, the church consisted of those who maintained the unity of the Catholic Church. To break this unity was to place oneself outside the communion of the church:

> Whoever breaks with the church and enters on an adulterous union cuts himself off from the promises made to the church, and he who turns his back on the church of Christ will not come to the rewards of Christ: he is an alien, a worldling, an enemy. You cannot have God for your Father if you no longer have the church for your mother. If there was any escape for one who was outside the ark of Noah, there will be as much for one who is found to be outside the church.[16]

Novatian and the five presbyters whom Cyprian excommunicated broke from the church to oppose Cornelius and Cyprian, therefore leaving the source (*origo*) that God had ordained.

With lapsed laypeople Cyprian and the African bishops took a moderate position to accommodate the many lapsed clamoring to return to the church. However, Cyprian was uncompromising when it came to

---

13. Cyprian, *Ep.* 55.19.

14. Burns, *Cyprian*, 75.

15. Cyprian, *Ep.* 59.9.

16. Cyprian, *Unit. eccl.* 6.1: "Quisque ab ecclesia segregatus adulterae iungitur, a promissis ecclesiae separatur, nec perveniet ad Christi praemia qui relinquit ecclesiam Christi: alienus est, profanus est, hostis est. Habere iam non potest Deum patrem qui ecclesiam non habet matrem. Si potuit evadere quisque extra arcam Noe fuit, et qui extra ecclesiam foris fuerit evadet."

those he felt were schismatics or heretics because he believed the sins of heresy and schism to be greater than the sin of apostasy. In *De unitate* Cyprian explains point by point why he holds this to be the case: First, the lapsed have sinned but are now doing penance and seeking the mercy of God, while the schismatics are continuing in their rebellion by remaining outside the church. Second, the lapsed were coerced into sinning but are now appealing to the mercy of the church by doing their prescribed penance. The schismatics, on the other hand, willfully left the church and remain in rebellion. Third, the lapsed have hurt only themselves in their fall, but the schismatics hurt many because they sever the unity of the church. Fourth, the lapsed sinned once, but the schismatics are continuing to sin each day by remaining outside the church. Lastly, the lapsed can become martyrs and receive a crown. The schismatics, because they are outside the church, cannot become martyrs or receive the rewards prepared for the church.[17]

However, when it came to lapsed bishops or presbyters Cyprian held a higher standard than for layfolk. When two Spanish congregations sought Cyprian's advice in deciding if their former bishops who had lapsed during the recent persecution should be reinstated as Bishop Stephen of Rome had ordered, Cyprian disagreed. In Cyprian's view, a lay person who had lapsed could be received back into the fellowship of the church in his or her former status, but a member of the episcopate who sinned could be admitted back into the church only as a lay person. In his reply to the Spanish churches, Cyprian told them that they had indeed made the proper decision in consecrating two new bishops, Felix and Sabinus, as replacements for the lapsed clerics Basilides and Maretial:

> It is therefore useless for such to attempt to lay claim to episcopal office for themselves. For it is more than obvious that men of such character are incapable of presiding over the church of Christ, nor is it right that they should offer sacrifices to God. And this is especially so since some time ago now our colleague and fellow bishop Cornelius, peacemaker and man of justice and, by the grace of the Lord, blessed with the dignity of martyrdom, joined with us and with every one of the bishops throughout the world in decreeing that it was indeed possible for men of such character to be admit-

---

17. *Unit. eccl.* 19.

ted to do penance but that they were to be debarred from holding
clerical office and episcopal rank.[18]

There are two things worth noting here. First, that Bishop Cornelius,
now martyred, had agreed with Cyprian on the issue of disqualifying
lapsed clerics speaks to the relationship and agreement between Cyprian
and the former bishop of Rome. It also suggests that, at least from
Cyprian's perspective, Bishop Stephen was the innovator when he chose
to reinstate the Spanish bishops. (However, Cyprian does admit in his
letter to the clergy of Spain that Basilides deceived Stephen by present-
ing himself as a victim.) Second, Cyprian's view regarding the treatment
of lapsed clergy would influence later generations of African Christians,
particularly the Donatists. Cyprian and many after him believed that
clergy who had a lapse in faith were left with a stain that disqualified
them from future ministry; Cyprian therefore insists that believers separate themselves from such ministers "since infidelity ought to be given no
advancement in the house of God."[19] Furthermore, Cyprian insists that to
keep communion with such "delinquents" makes one a sharer in their sin.
Citing Exodus 19:22 and 28:43 and Leviticus 21:17, Cyprian argues that
these fallen clerics will contaminate others if allowed to continue in their
positions. As a result, any sacrament they perform is not only invalid but
also has the potential to infect others:

> And the faithful are not to beguile themselves with notions that
> while they are in communion with a bishop who is a sinner and
> acquiesce in their church leader's wrongful and unlawful exercise
> of episcopal powers, they can remain themselves untouched by the
> infection of his office. For God in His strict justice issues us with
> His warning through the prophet Hosea in these words: "Their
> sacrifices are like the bread of mourning; all who eat of them shall
> be defiled."[20]

18. Cyprian, *Ep.* 67.6.3: "Frustra tales episcopatum sibi usurpare conantur, cum
manifestius sit eiusmodi homines nec ecclesiae Christi posse praeesse nec Deo sacrificia
offerre debere, maxime cum iam pridem nobiscum et cum omnibus omnino episcopis
in toto mundo constitutis etiam Cornelius collega noster, sacerdos pacificus ac iustus et
martyrio quoque dignatione domini honoratus, decreverit eiusmodi homines ad paenitentiam quidem agendam posse admitti, ab ordinatione autem cleri atque sacerdotali
honore prohiberi."

19. Cyprian, *Ep.* 72.2: "non tamen debet in domo fidei perfidia promoveri."

20. Cyprian, *Ep.* 67.3: "Nec sibi plebs blandiatur quasi inmunis esse a contagio delicti
possit cum sacerdote peccatore communicans et ad iniustum atque inlicitum praepositi

This conviction concerning the connection between the moral worthiness of clergy and the effect of their sacramental acts was to have grave consequences for the future of North African Christianity.

BAPTISM OR REBAPTISM: CYPRIAN AND STEPHEN

Around May 12, 254, Stephen succeeded to the episcopal chair of Bishop Lucius. Although none of Bishop Stephen's letters have survived, the gist of his teaching can be ascertained from the letters of Bishop Firmilian of Caesarea and Bishop Cyprian of Carthage. Even before the dispute over the reinstatement of the Spanish clerics, a rift developed between the sees of Carthage and Rome. At some point, members from Novatian's churches began seeking readmission to the North African churches under Cyprian's jurisdiction. As a result, Bishop Magus writes to Cyprian (circa 253) asking his opinion about the baptism of those who returned from Novatian churches.[21] Cyprian refuses to call what these people received in Novatian's community a baptism; for him it is only a "dipping"; persons coming from Novatian or any heretical group must be baptized in the true church. Citing Ephesians 4:4–5 Cyprian insists that there is only one church and one baptism. Baptism outside the one church is invalid because remission of sin cannot happen outside the church. Since those "baptized" in heretical or schismatic bodies never received a true baptism, they are not getting rebaptized, in Cyprian's view, when they are being baptized in the true church. Magus' letter also shows that he and other African bishops did not share this position in the early stages of the debate and so did not (re)baptize those entering the church from groups deemed heretical or schismatic. As a result, Cyprian convened a council of African bishops to resolve the issue. This council reached these conclusions: 1) Persons "dipped" outside the church have been stained with profane waters, so they must come to the true church and be baptized. 2) Contrary to Stephen's teaching, heretical baptism cannot be made valid by the laying on of hands to receive the Holy Spirit. 3) Any priest who ministered in an heretical body must be received as a layman when he returns to the true church.[22] Reporting these results to Stephen, Cyprian

---

sui episcopatum consensum suum commodans, quando per Osee prophetam commineetur et dicat censura divina: 'Sacrificia eorum tamquam panis luctus, omnes qui manducant ea contaminabuntur.'"

21. Cyprian, *Ep.71*. Clarke dates this letter to the middle of 253.

22. Cyprian, *Ep. 71*.

courteously tells the bishop of Rome that he, Cyprian, is not trying to lay down a law for everyone to follow but that each priest has the freedom to do what he thinks is best, since each priest in the end will be accountable to God. Stephen responds to Cyprian's letter with sharp disagreement, insisting that, no matter where baptism was performed, it is valid as long as the divine names are pronounced. Stephen further argues it does not matter who administers the baptism for its effect is derived from Jesus Christ and the faith of the person being baptized. He also contends that schismatic or heretical baptism confers the grace of Christ but not the gift of the Holy Spirit. Evans assesses the Roman position as follows:

> It appears that Stephen and the Roman clergy adopted two lines of interpretation at one or another time. On the one hand the imposition of the bishop's hand was seen as an analogy to the practice whereby Christians who had committed post-baptismal sin were received to the church's communion after evidence of their penitence. On the other hand the rationale was developed that the bishop was completing the act of initiation begun in water baptism and in the imposition of his hand was imparting the gift of the Holy Spirit.[23]

The reception of the Holy Spirit around the sacrament of baptism was understood differently in Rome and North Africa. Cyprian believed that the believer received the Holy Spirit immediately at baptism, while Stephen held that the baptismal candidate received the Holy Spirit when the bishop, after having baptized, laid hands on him or her. Stephen therefore allowed members of Novatian's group to be admitted to the church of Rome without the repetition of water baptism.

This rapidly turned into more than an intellectual debate. Stephen wrote to Cyprian instructing him to follow the Roman teaching on baptism on pain of excommunication not only for Cyprian but for any church that followed him.[24] Unlike Cornelius before him, Stephen believed that he had the authority to make such demands. Concerning Stephen's view of authority, Evans notes:

> Stephen was much incensed by the refusal of Cyprian and the African bishops to follow him in his policy and adopted a provocative argument for bringing the recalcitrant bishops into line.

23. Evans, *One and Holy*, 60.
24. We get this from the letter he wrote to Bishop Firmilian, Cyprian, *Ep.* 67.5.

> In the history of the Roman episcopate he was the first, so far as
> we know, to appeal to his own particular position as successor to
> Peter on whom the Lord built his church, the first to claim thereby
> a "primacy" entitling him to be obeyed by other bishops.[25]

Cyprian, however, did not accept Stephen's or any other bishop's authority
over himself. He did believe that bishops could meet in council to decide
points of discipline, but he also believed that every bishop had the right
to make his own decisions regarding the church over which he presided,
since he is Christ's representative and will in the end have to be accountable to God.[26]

The division thus brought about was bitter, and Bishop Stephen refused to see an African delegation sent by Cyprian to discuss the issue.[27]
Both men held firm in their beliefs, maintaining that they were each following the tradition of the church. Stephen asserted that his policy on
baptism was a continuous tradition of the Roman church, conforming to
that church's practice in receiving Marcionites.[28] Cyprian likewise maintained that the baptism or rebaptism of heretics was a consistent policy of
the African churches, begun with Agrippinus, affirmed by Tertullian, and
continued to his own day. He responded to Stephen:

> But whereas no heresy whatsoever nor indeed any schism, being
> outside the church, can have the sanctification and saving power
> of baptism, yet the unyielding obstinacy of our brother Stephen
> has now hardened to such a degree that he insists that sons are
> born of God even from the baptism of Marcion, and from that
> of Valentinus as well as of Apelles and all the other blasphemers
> against God the Father, and he argues that forgiveness of sins is
> there granted in the name of Jesus Christ where men blaspheme
> the Father and against Christ, the Lord God.[29]

25. Evans, *One and Holy*, 60.

26. Firmilian's letter to Cyprian, *Ep.*74.

27. Cyprian, *Ep.* 75.25.

28. Evans, *One and Holy*, 69.

29. *Ep.* 74.7.3: "Cum vero nulla omino haeresis, sed neque aliquod schisma habere
salutaris baptismi sanctificationem foris possit, intantum Stephani fratris nostri obstina-
tio dura prorupit, ut etiam de Marcionis baptismo, item Valentini et Appelletis et cetero-
rum blasphemantium Deum patrem contendat filios deo nasci, et illic in nomine Iesu
Christi dicat remissionem peccatorum dari ubi blasphematur in Patrem et dominum et
deum Christum."

Cyprian could not imagine a person outside the church administering a valid baptism. So, as pointed out above, he insists in several letters that he is not rebaptizing persons but rather that, "we say that those who come thence are not rebaptized among us, but are baptized."[30] A similar tradition of rebaptizing heretics also existed in several churches in Asia Minor. In a letter of support for Cyprian, bishop Firmilian challenges Stephen's arguments that the use of the divine name is sufficient to make heretical baptism valid and that a person's faith outside the church is acceptable:

> But there is more absurdity: they consider there is no need to in-
> quire who it is who has administered baptism, arguing that the
> person baptized can have obtained grace merely by the invocation
> of the Trinity. It follows that this is wisdom which Paul writes is
> to be found in those who are perfected! This is what the man who
> has been perfected in the church and is wise must believe and
> defend, vis. that the mere invocation of these names suffices for
> obtaining the remission of sins and the sanctification of baptism.
> But, in fact, these names are effective when, and only when, both
> the person who baptizes possesses the Holy Spirit and the baptism
> itself also has not been established without the Spirit. And they
> further contend that, whatever the manner of the baptism outside
> the church, a man may obtain the grace of baptism by virtue of his
> personal faith and disposition. That, too, is obviously preposter-
> ous, as though a corrupt disposition could have power to draw
> down to itself from heaven the sanctification of the righteous, or a
> false faith the truth of believers.[31]

Firmilian and the Asian bishops were in agreement with Cyprian and the African bishops with a few minor differences. As Burns points out, Firmilian was careful not only to mention the image of Noah's ark but also to remind the reader that those persons outside the ark drowned, em-

30. *Ep.* 71.1.3: "Nos autem dicimus eos qui inde veniunt non rebaptizari apud nos, sed baptizari."

31. *Ep.* 75.9.1: "Illud quoque absurdum quod non putant quarendum esse quis sit ille qui baptizaverit, eo quod qui baptizatus sit gratiam consequi potuerit invocata trinitate nominum patris et filii et spiritus sancti. Deinde haec erit sapientia quam scribit Paulus esse in his qui perfecti sunt, ut qui est in ecclesia perfectus et sapiens hoc aut defendat aut credat, quod invocatio haec nominum nuda sufficiat ad remissionem peccatorum et baptismi sanctificationem, cum haec tunc utique proficiant, quando et qui baptizat habet spiritum sanctum et baptisma quoque ipsum non sit sine spiritu constitutum, Sed dicunt eum qui quomodocumque foris baptizatur mente et fide sua baptismi gratiam consequi posse. Quid et ipsum sine dubio ridiculum est, quasi de caelo adducere ad se possit aut mens prava iustorum sanctificationem aut fides falsa credentium veritatem."

phasizing the penalty for rebellion. Moreover, Bishop Firmilian laid even more emphasis than Cyprian on the church as both the bride of Christ and the sole mother of God's children. Lastly, Firmilian also warned that schismatics admitted to communion without proper baptism put themselves in grave danger in coming into contact with the body of Christ through the eucharist.[32]

THE AFRICAN BISHOPS ON THE BAPTISM OF HERETICS, 256 CE

In the two years preceding his death, Cyprian wrote letters and convened several councils to discuss the issue of the baptism of schismatics and heretics. After the bitter dispute with Stephen of Rome, Cyprian convened another African council, possibly with the intention of unifying his position in Africa. This council met at Carthage on September 1, 256, with eighty-seven bishops in attendance. According to Monceaux, Cyprian had perfected the ancient Tironian system of taking notes and thus was able to record this council with great accuracy.[33] During the council each bishop in order of seniority gave his opinion about the baptism of heretics. One argument repeated at least twenty times drew on Ephesians 4:4-5, which Cyprian had cited previously in his debate with Stephen: "There is one body and one Spirit, just as you were called to the one hope of your calling, one Lord, one faith, one baptism." The African bishops reasoned that if the Church is one and baptism is one, then how can there possibly be two different and valid baptisms? One has to be false. Concerning this point, Hortensianus of Lares states:

> Let either these presumptuous ones, or those who favor heretics, consider how many baptisms there are—we claim for the church one baptism, which we know not except in the church—or how can they baptize any one in the name of Christ, whom Christ himself declares to be his adversaries?[34]

The African bishops also discussed the identity of the true church and its sacraments and its distinction from the false church and its false

---

32. Burns, *Cyprian*, 121. On the last point, see 1 Cor. 11:27.

33. Monceaux, *Histoire*, 2:63.

34. Migne, S. Cypriani Opera. *Sententiae* 21: "Hortensianus a Laribus dixit: Quot sint baptismi viderint aut praesumptores aut fautores haereticorum; nos unum baptisma, quod non nisi in ecclesia novimus, ecclesiae vindicamus. Aut quomodo possunt in nomine Christi aliquem baptizare quos ipse Christus dicit adversarios suos esse?"

sacraments. Three examples will illustrate their reasoning. Privatianus of Sufetula argues:

> Let him who says that heretics have the power of baptizing say first who founded heresy. For if heresy is of God, it also may have the divine indulgence. But if it is not from God, how can it either have the grace of God or confer it upon anyone?[35]

Secundinus of Carpi asks:

> Are heretics Christians or not? If they are Christians, why are they not in the church of God? If they are not Christians, how can they make Christians? Or whither will tend the Lord's discourse, when he says, "He that is not with me is against me, and he who does not gather with me scatters"? Whence it appears plainly that upon strange children, and on the offspring of Antichrist, the Holy Spirit cannot descend only by imposition of hands, since it is manifest that heretics do not have baptism.[36]

Donatus of Cibalina declares: "I know one church and her one baptism. If there is any who says that the grace of baptism is with heretics, he must first show and prove that the church is among them."[37]

The African bishops contend that the church is one and that it possesses one baptism and one faith. For Cyprian and the other African bishops, heretics and schismatics are completely excluded from the church, and Cyprian argues this forcefully in his *De unitate* and his letters. However, the total exclusion of schismatics and heretics was a weakness in Cyprian's ecclesiology. Cyprian did not distinguish between the two in drawing the boundaries of the church. He even likened schismatic Christians like Novatian to the anti-Christ.

---

35. Ibid., *Sententiae* 20: "Privatianus a Sufetula dixit: Qui haereticos potestatem baptizandi habere dicit, dicat prius quis haeresim condiderit. Si enim haeresis a Deo est, habere et indulgentiam divinam potest. Si vero a Deo non est, quomodo gratiam Dei aut habere aut conferre alicui potest?"

36. Ibid., *Sententiae* 24: "Gaius Secuudinus a Carpis dixit: Haeretici christiani sunt, an non? Si christiani sunt, cur in ecclesia Dei non sunt? Si christiani non sunt, quomodo christianos faciunt? Aut quo pertinebit sermo Domini dicentis (Matth. xii,30) : 'Qui non est mecum, adversus me est, et qui non mecum colligit spargit.' Unde constat super filios alienos et soboles antichristi Spiritum Sanctum per manus impositionem tantummodo non posse descendere, cum manifestum sit haereticos baptisma non habere."

37. Ibid., *Sententiae* 55: "Donatus a Cibalina dixit: Ego unam ecclesiam et unum baptisma eius novi. Si est qui dicat esse apud haereticos baptismi gratiam, ante est ut ostendat et probet esse illic ecclesiam."

Stephen's ecclesiology likewise failed to make this distinction between heretics clearly outside the bounds of Christian teaching and schismatics nearer to the Catholic Church. As a result, he was said to have taught that even persons coming from such groups as those of Marcion, Apelles, and Valentinus could have a valid baptism if they just recited the divine names or had hands laid on them by the bishop. This opened him up to the criticism from both Cyprian and Firmilian that he placed custom over truth.

Cyprian's main goal was to bring about unity. However, in doing so, he drew too sharp a line for the boundary of the church, though not as sharp as Tertullian before him or Novatian in his own time, but sharp enough that he excluded many who might have been restored to the unity of the church. On the other hand, the strength of Cyprian's ecclesiology was that he found a way to allow the body of saints to include sinners forgiven of grave sins and admitted back into the church. The only requirement was that they be subject to their bishop in fulfilling their penance.

6

The Great Persecution and
the Rise of the Donatists

303-305
BCE

EVENTS LEADING UP TO THE GREAT PERSECUTION OF 303 CE

WHILE CYPRIAN HAD REGULARLY corresponded with Christians throughout the empire on a variety of issues so that his literature is available to us, the literary sources from bishops who immediately followed him are limited. For example, we do not have any letters from bishops Majorinus, Donatus, or Caecilian. Moreover, the sources we do have display great bitterness between the dissenting parties. To be fair to both sides, we must attempt to penetrate beneath this highly polemical and prejudicial rhetoric as we seek to understand the ecclesiastical divisions brought about in Africa by Diocletian's persecution and the challenges that emerged from the novelty of a Christian emperor, Constantine.

After the deaths of Stephen in 257 and Cyprian in 258, Rome and North Africa continued their respective traditions of baptism and church discipline. Africans continued into the fourth century their practice of re-baptizing schismatics and heretics. However, during this period of peace and prosperity (260–300) divisive theological issues remained dormant as Christians throughout the empire began to rebuild their communities and ascend the career ladders of Roman officialdom. According to Eusebius, more and more Christians were afforded high positions in the government, and churches received members from the upper as well as the lower classes of society. As a result of this peace between church and empire, Christians increased in number, new churches were erected, and Christians worshiped openly.[1] However, as Frend notes, the possibility of persecution was never far removed. For example, if Christians refused to

upper-class Xians

---

1. Eusebius, *Hist. eccl.* 8.1.

sacrifice on public occasions, the law still provided that they could be put to death, though for the most part this threat did not materialize during this period. The emperors who succeeded Valerian—Probus (276–282), Carus (282–283), and Carinus (283–285)—were too engaged in military exploits outside the empire to pay much attention to the Christians.[2]

Eusebius maintains that the Christian population at large did not appreciate the divine favor granted them and therefore became arrogant and began mistreating one another. Thus he, like Cyprian before him, credits the persecution of his day to God's judgment on a disobedient church.[3] The Latin writer Lactantius offers a different though no less theological account of the origin of Diocletian's persecution, but beneath the surface of Lactantius' narrative indications may be seen of more secular concerns that turned the emperor into Christianity's fiercest persecutor.

At the beginning of his reign, Diocletian's main concern was to secure the borders of the empire. Rome's territory had grown too large, Diocletian believed, to be ruled by one man. So he divided the empire in half, calling one Maximian to assist him, designating his imperial colleague as Caesar in 285 and then as Augustus in 286 and assigning him the responsibility of governing the western provinces. In 293, Diocletian created a four-fold imperial government, the tetrarchy, assigning east and west to two Augusti, each of whom had a Caesar to assist him. Diocletian chose Galerius as Caesar in the east, and Maximian chose Constantius, Constantine's father, as Caesar in the west. All four tetrarchs were experienced military men. This proved to be both a blessing and a curse to the empire. On the one hand, they succeeded in keeping Rome safe from external threats; on the other, as Lactantius reports, each man in an attempt to outdo the other "strove to maintain a much more considerable military force than any sole emperor had done in times past."[4] Thus the citizens of Rome were burdened by both the threat of civil war between competing princes and excessive taxes to support not only the military but also Diocletian's many building projects. In this atmosphere, Diocletian simply ignored the churches for the first nineteen years of his reign. According to Lactantius, this changed when Diocletian sought the advice of the Roman gods concerning his future.

2. Frend, *Martyrdom*, 108.

3. Eusebius, *Hist. eccl.* 8.1.

4. Lactantius, *Mort.* 7.

Lactantius recounts that while sacrificing several animals, Diocletian, according to the usual practice, had the soothsayers examine the sacrificial victims' livers to get a prediction concerning himself. After several failed attempts, the chief soothsayer Tages informed him that the soothsayers could not get a reading because there were "profane persons" obstructing the rite. Diocletian took this to mean the Christians and became outraged. In his anger he ordered everyone in his palace to sacrifice to the Roman gods or be scourged. He then ordered soldiers in his army to sacrifice or be dismissed from service.[5] These actions would have satisfied Diocletian, Lactantius maintains, had not Galerius nagged him to persecute the Christians further. While the Augustus wintered in Bithynia (289–90), Galerius, who was his son-in-law as well as Caesar, did his best to incite Diocletian to persecute the Christians.[6] Diocletian resisted his advice at first, believing the exclusion of Christians from the palace and the army was sufficient. However, at Galerius' insistence, Diocletian sought the advice of some of his civil magistrates and military commanders. Because many of them feared Galerius, they took the latter's side and advised that the Christians should be persecuted. Diocletian, however, was still unwilling to take this step without the advice and approval of the gods. So the emperors consulted Apollo at Didyma in 302. Now at this service, the person in charge is reported to have said "the just of the earth," that is, the Christians, stopped them from getting a good reading.[7] At this attack on the Christians, Diocletian finally agreed (reluctantly) to persecute them. But even in his acquiescence, he did not want to shed any blood, thereby making martyrs, but only to "persuade" Christians through the necessary force (torture) to quit their stubbornness and acknowledge the Roman gods.

He and Galerius chose a special day for the start of this undertaking: the day of the festival of the god *Terminus*, as if to indicate that the Christian religion would finally be terminated. With that in mind, their first edict demanded that churches were to be razed to the ground, scriptures to be confiscated and burned, and obstinate Christians to lose their places of

---

5. Lactantius, *Mort.* 10. The martydrom of the soldier Maximilian may have been a result of this decision: Musurillo, *Acts*, 244–49.

6. Lactantius informs us that Galerius got his hatred of Christians from his mother: *Mort.* 11.

7. Fox, *Pagans and Christians*, 595.

honor and be denied their civil rights.[8] When the first edict was enforced, government agents immediately tore down the church in Nicomedia and put Christian scriptures in a pile and burned them. Despite this, the first edict was not stern enough for Galerius, so he had some of his servants set Diocletian's palace on fire and, in a move similar to that of Nero centuries before, blamed the Christians for this atrocity. This had the desired effect, as the very name "Christian" became hated among the people.[9] Diocletian, now having his mind set against the Christians, ordered three more edicts, each one more severe than the previous one, until he finally allowed for the death penalty for those who refused to sacrifice.[10] From the Roman perspective, the Christians' offense lay in the obstinacy of their beliefs, and so the government's aim was coercive rather than punitive. Unlike other condemned criminals set for execution, they would be released if they recanted.[11] Unfortunately, when Christians resisted, some of the emperors, such as Galerius and Maximian Daia, displayed the utmost cruelty in their efforts to force Christians to comply.[12]

WHERE IS THE CHURCH IN NORTH AFRICA?

It is not the purpose of this work to cover the effects of the Great Persecution throughout the empire;[13] but in North Africa (circa 303/4), local authorities enforced the ban on Christian gatherings and demanded the surrender of sacred texts. During this time, Bishop Fundanus of Abitinia, a town in North Africa, became a *traditor* (that is, he surrendered the sacred texts) and so forfeited the right to lead his congregation. His congregation continued to meet under the direction of a presbyter named Saturninus at the home of the lector Emeritus. During a worship service, the imperial authorities surprised this small congregation and arrested its members for holding an unlawful assembly. They were immediately hauled off to the neighboring town of Carthage, where the Roman

8. Eusebius, *Hist. eccl.* 8.2.

9. Lactantius, *Mort.* 14.

10. Tilley insists that "the fourth edict of this persecution was not issued by Diocletian, but Galerius during Diocletian's illness." *Stories*, xxix.

11. Gaddis, *No Crime*, 35.

12. For the cruelty exhibited during the persecution, see Eusebius, *Hist. eccl.* 8–10 and Lactantius, *Mort.* 1–52.

13. For an excellent study on the Great Persecution througout the empire, see Frend, *Martyrdom*, 477-521.

authorities had accommodations to house prisoners.[14] After admitting to having met for "divine worship," the confessors were tortured one by one, but they all remained steadfast in their faith. The narrator gives the following account of Emeritus under torture:

> Once Emeritus was charged, the proconsul said, "Were assemblies held in your home against the order of the emperor?" Emeritus, filled with the Holy Spirit, said to him, "We did hold the Lord's supper in my home." In reply the proconsul said, "Why did you permit them to enter?" He responded, "Because they are my brothers and sisters and I could not prevent them from doing so." Then the proconsul said, "You should have prevented them from doing so." In response Emeritus said, "I could not because we cannot go without the Lord's supper." At once the proconsul ordered him to be stretched out on the rack, and once stretched out, to be tortured. After new executioners came on duty, while he was suffering heavy blows, he said, "I beseech you, O Christ, come to my aid. You wretches are the ones acting against the command of God (cf. Acts 5:29)." The proconsul interrupted, "You should not have admitted them." Emeritus responded, "I could not but admit my brothers and sisters." Then the sacrilegious proconsul said, "But the order of the emperors and the Caesars takes priority." In reply the most pious martyr said, "God is greater—and not the emperors. I pray, O Christ. Praise to you. Give me endurance." The proconsul interrupted him as he prayed, "Do you have any scriptures in your home?" He responded, "I have them but they are in my heart (2 Cor. 3.3)."[15]

In spite of repeated interrogations, Emeritus and the other confessors persisted in their faith and boldly repeated that famous phrase *Christianus sum* ("I am a Christian"). Toward the end of this account, the narrator informs the reader that Mensurius, the bishop of Carthage, and his deacon Caecilian were accused of preventing these confessors from receiving food brought to them by their families and friends.[16] These confessors soon became martyrs by dying of starvation in prison. Before they succumbed, however, they asked the faithful to excommunicate everyone who associated with the evil bishop Mensurius and his deacon Caecilian (sec. 20). The confessors believed such persons merited eternal

14. Tilley, *Bible*, 9.

15. Translation from Tilley, *Stories*, 37.

16. Tilley, *Bible*, 9.

punishment. Moreover, in a view similar to Cyprian's, they argued that persons who maintained communion with the *traditores* would be contaminated, and therefore would not participate with them in the joys of heaven.[17] Within a few years of the confessor's pronouncement against him, Bishop Mensurius died, and the episcopal seat at Carthage became vacant. During the period between Cyprian and the Great Persecution, Christianity flourished in the countryside of Numidia, allowing the bishops increased importance. At some point, the bishops of Numidia gained the right to consecrate the bishop of Carthage. Thus, upon the death of Bishop Mensurius of Carthage, seventy Numidian bishops led by Bishop Secundus of Tigisis went to Carthage in hopes of electing a new bishop.[18] When they arrived in Carthage, they were surprised to find that the election had already taken place and that the deacon Caecilian had been ordained bishop of Carthage. The church population, as well as the bishops of Numidia, were furious at Caecilian's consecration. They argued that Caecilian was consecrated by only three bishops instead of the usual twelve, and that one of them, Felix of Apthungi, was a *traditor*. Moreover, Caecilian's involvement in the starvation of the Abitinian martyrs and their demand to have him excommunicated made his choice as bishop unacceptable.[19] As Tilley notes, "this issue was not only the betrayal of the Bible by Caecilian's consecrator, but also Caecilian's own acquiescence in the destruction of the men and women who embodied the words of the Bible in their lives, the Abitinian martyrs."[20] Thus, the initial seeds of the bitter and enduring animosity among Christians in North Africa were the events surrounding the mistreatment of the Abitinian martyrs in 303/4 and the election of Caecilian as bishop of Carthage.

The African historian Bishop Optatus of Melevis, however, writing around 384, attributes the split between the two churches to moral shortcomings, to anger, jealousy, and greed:

> No one is unaware that this took place at Carthage after the ordination of Caecilian, and indeed through some factious woman or other called Lucilla, who, while the church was still tranquil and

17. *Acta Saturnini* (PL 8:703): "Si quis traditoribus communicaverit, nobiscum partem in regnis caelestibus non habebit."

18. Frend, *Early Church*, 127–28. Frend contends that since the time of Cyprian the primate of Numidia had the right of consecrating the new primate of Carthage.

19. Tilley, *Bible*, 10.

20. Ibid.

the peace had not yet been shattered by the whirlwinds of persecution, was unable to bear the rebuke of the archdeacon Caecilian. She was said to kiss the bone of some martyr or other—if, that is, he was a martyr—before the spiritual food and drink, and, since she preferred to the saving cup the bone of some dead man, who if he was a martyr had not yet been confirmed as one, she was rebuked and went away in angry humiliation. As she raged and grieved, a storm of persecution suddenly arose to prevent her submitting to discipline.[21]

Bishop Optatus goes on to say that after peace was restored to the church, Lucilla along with two other men, Botrus and Celestius, who had hoped to be elected bishop, withdrew from the communion of the church at the announcement of Caecilian's election. Moreover, in addition to Lucilla's departure from the church, Optatus maintains that she was instrumental in having her domestic Majorinus elected.[22] Nonetheless, even if Optatus' account of Lucilla is true and she helped Caecilian's rival get elected, three facts remain that are damning to Caecilian: first, that he hurried to secure his election before the Numidian bishops could take part in it as they were accustomed to doing; second, the unproven but also unrefuted accusation that a member or members of his faction murdered the man set in Caecilian's place until his right to be bishop was decided; and third, and most damaging of all, that as a deacon Caecilian prevented the Abitinian martyrs from receiving food from their families.

   It seems clear that the strong tradition of respect both for the wishes of the confessors and martyrs and for Cyprian's teaching concerning lapsed clerics survived among many Christians in North Africa. The Carthaginian and Numidian lower classes formed an alliance against Caecilian and any bishop who supported him. Like Cyprian before him, Bishop Secundus convened a council in 312 to settle the matter, apparently enforcing the tradition of the Numidian bishops since the time of Cyprian. As in the councils held by their hero and martyr Cyprian, each

---

21. Optatus, *Schis.*15–16 (PL 11:778): "Nemo qui nesciat, per Lucillam scilicet, nescio quam feminam factiosam: quae ante concussam persecutionis turbinibus pacem, dum adhuc in tranquillo esset ecclesia, cum correptionem archidiaconi Caeciliani ferre non posset, quae ante spiritalem cibum et potum, os nescio cuius martyris, si tamen martyris, libare dicebatur: et cum praeponeret calici salutari os nescio cuius hominis mortui, etsi martyris sed necdum vindicati correpta, cum confusione discessit irata. Irascenti et dolenti, ne disciplinae succumberet occurrit subito persecutionis enata tempestas."

22. Optatus, *Schis.*, 1.9: "domesticus Lucillae."

bishop brought forth his view in a short speech. The record of the council has not survived, but the gist of the meeting can be summed up in the account of Bishop Marcian:

> In his gospel the Lord says, "I am the true vine and my Father is the husbandman. Every branch in me that does not bear fruit he cuts off and casts away; and every branch that bears fruit, he cleanses." Thus, unfruitful branches are to be cut off and cast aside. So *thurificti*, *traditores*, and those who being in schism are ordained by *traditores* cannot remain with the church of God, unless they are reconciled through penance with wailing acknowledgment [of their faith]. Hence, no one ought to communicate with Caecilian, who has been ordained by *traditores* in schism.[23]

This citation clearly shows that the opponents of Caecilian were following in Cyprian's steps, in that they considered lapsed clergy who refused to do penance as schismatics. Like Cyprian, the Numidians and Carthaginians did not exclude these clerics from the church indefinitely but insisted that they must do penance before being admitted back into the fellowship of the church. We can assume that, in accord with Cyprian's views, such clerics after penance would be readmitted to the church, but only as lay members. In accord with this stance, this council and another one held the same year (312) condemned Caecilian and placed a new bishop in his position. The Numidian and Carthaginian lower classes consecrated an interim bishop in Caecilian's place; but Caecilian's party is supposed to have murdered him in his own meetinghouse.[24] When the Numidian bishops held a council to elect a new bishop, Caecilian requested that they consecrate him a second time, but they elected Majorinus instead.[25] Caecilian, however, refused to relinquish his see, and in 313, shortly after his appointment, Bishop Majorinus died. He was then re-

---

23. Frend, *Donatist*, 20. *Liber contra Fulgentium Donatistam*, 26 (PL 43:774): "In evangelio suo Dominus ait, 'Ego sum vitis vera, et Pater meus agricola; omnem palmitem in me non afferentem fructum, excidet et proiciet; et omnem manentem in me et fructum ferentem, purgat illum.' Sicut ergo palmites infructuosi amputati proiciuntur, ita thurificati, traditores, et qui in schismate a traditoribus ordinantur manere in ecclesia Dei non possunt, nisi cognito ululatu suo per poenitentiam reconcilientur. Unde Ceciliano in schismate a traditoribus ordinato non communicare oportet."

24. Elliott, *Constantine*, 81.

25. Frend, *Donatist*, 19.

placed by Bishop Donatus, from whom the opponents of Caecilian took their name.[26]

Thus, by 313 disputed elections, violence, and political maneuvering had sealed the rift between the two parties. Consequently, as long as Christianity was a force in North Africa, it was divided into two distinct groups, one associated with Bishop Caecilian and backed by the imperial authorities and the other named after Majorinus' successor Donatus the Great.

Donatists vs. Caecilian's party

There is little doubt that many Africans disliked Caecilian and believed he had a part in the mistreatment of the Abitinian martyrs, but neither side was blameless, and indeed both sides accused each other of having lapsed clergy. For example, Optatus of Milevis maintained in his account that Secundus, the very bishop who led the charge against Caecilian, was himself a man of questionable character and possibly a *traditor*.[27]

Nevertheless, neither side would compromise and each group accused the other of causing a schism. In addition, Bishop Donatus, following Cyprian, continued the tradition of baptizing or rebaptizing schismatics and heretics in such numbers that Bishop Miltiades of Rome, himself an African, in October of 313 pronounced him guilty of causing a schism.[28] This renewed tensions between Rome and North Africa over the issue of baptism that had been dormant since the Decian persecution. However, this time North African Christians were not unified: members of Caecilian's group sided with Rome on this issue, while the group led by Bishop Donatus followed the African tradition as laid down by Agrippinus, Tertullian, and Cyprian.

26. For a discussion on the identity of Donatus the Great and Donatus of Casae Nigrae, see Chapman, "Donatus." He believes that they were the same person. Frend also believes that they were the same person, while Monceaux believes they were two different people (*Histoire*, 5:99–105). I belive that they were two different persons, on the grounds that the Donatists themselves insisted that there were two different people at the conference in 411. Donatus was also a popular African name.

27. Optatus, *Schis.* 1.14.2. Puripius alleges that since Secundus was released from jail without a stated reason, it may have been because he collaborated.

28. Frend, *Donatist*, 15. Regarding Miltiades' African heritage, see Fage, *History*, 468.

EMPEROR CONSTANTINE AND
NORTH AFRICAN CHRISTIANITY

As the schism in Africa continued, Constantine defeated Maxentius in 312, bringing North Africa under his rule. Thus the new emperor was called upon to resolve a dispute that had been raging for several years. In his first response to the situation, Constantine sent a letter to Anulinus, the proconsul of Africa, instructing him to restore property to "the Catholic Church of the Christians," by which he meant the party of Caecilian.[29] According to the Donatists, Constantine was influenced against their party by his religious adviser Bishop Ossius of Corduba.[30] Thus, Constantine unintentionally exacerbated the situation. The Donatists became angry and appealed to Constantine to hear their case, insisting that they be given judges from Gaul. The emperor consented, but when the council was finally held, Bishop Miltiades of Rome took steps to control the outcome, as Drake observes:

> Unable, or unwilling, directly to jeopardize his relationship with the new ruler of Rome, Miltiades was equally unwilling to preside over a council of whose outcome he could not be certain. When the council opened in October, an additional fifteen bishops were present, all from Italy, all of his choosing.[31]

In addition, Miltiades inhibited the Donatists' ability to arbitrate their case by following "strict rules of evidence and argument as laid down for Roman civil proceedings."[32] The Donatists thus became so frustrated that they left the meeting in disgust without actually having presented their case. Bishop Miltiades declared Caecilian innocent by default.[33]

It is likely that Miltiades' mistreatment of the Donatists at the council he chaired as well as Constantine's policy of favoring Caecilian's party (whom he and posterity accorded the title of "Catholic") caused the emperor to feel obliged to give the Donatists another hearing. In addition, when he saw that he was in trouble with his policy of favoring the Catholics, Constantine bent over backwards to be fair to the Donatists.[34]

29. Drake, *Constantine*, 214.
30. Ibid., 217.
31. Ibid., 218.
32. Ibid., 219.
33. Ibid., 218–9.
34. Elliott, *Constantine*, 91.

Thus when the Donatists appealed to Constantine again, he convened a council at Arles in August 314, but again the ruling went against them.[35] At the conclusion of this meeting, Constantine believed that the Donatists had received a fair hearing and is on record as saying:

> What power of wickedness perseveres in their hearts! How often have they been overwhelmed already by me personally in a reply quite deserved by their own most shameful approaches! Truly, if they had cared to keep this before their eyes, they would not have introduced this appeal! They demand my judgment, while I await Christ's judgment. For I declare, as is the truth, that the bishop's judgment ought to be regarded as if the Lord himself were sitting in judgment.[36]

[handwritten margin note: Donatists series of appeals to Constantine]

But the Donatists persisted in their demands and appealed to the emperor once more. Before Constantine scheduled this final hearing with the Donatists, he told them that if they could prove one of their claims against Caecilian he would rule in their favor.[37] Nonetheless, justice eluded the Donatists yet again; before the meeting was held, Bishop Caecilian hurried away from Rome and returned to Carthage.[38] Soon Bishop Donatus followed and both returned to be greeted by rioting in the streets of the city.

Constantine had promised to go to Carthage and judge the situation personally, but he never did. With such political maneuvering and gamesmanship it is difficult to determine the facts in the case. I suggest the following scenario. First, it may very well be true that Bishop Caecilian was not ordained by a *traditor* but that someone in the Donatist camp falsified a document to try to prove that he was. Constantine's own investigation reported that the letter entered into evidence against Felix of Abthungi was determined to be a forgery by one Ingentius.[39] Nonetheless, even if Constantine's determination on this point was true, this does not mean that Caecilian and the Catholics were innocent of all the charges leveled against them, such as the mistreatment of the Abitinian martyrs, the murder of the interim bishop, and the rushed election of Caecilian that caused

35. Ibid., 112.

36. Translation by Elliott, *Constantine*, 88–89. See Maier, *Dossier*, documents 23, 25.

37. Elliott, *Constantine*, 90.

38. Optatus, (tr. Edwards) *Against the Donatists*, Appendix Two: "The Acquittal Proceedings of Felix Bishop Abthungi," 9.

39. Elliott, *Constantine*, 91.

the schism in the first place. If Caecilian was innocent of all these charges, why did he rush to hold his election before the Numidian bishops arrived, contrary to the custom at the time? I suggest that the reason for his hurried election was that Caecilain was guilty of one or more of these charges and knew that he would not be confirmed by the Numidian bishops. If this is the case, one can understand why the schism lasted as long as it did and why the Donatists were persistent in seeking justice by repeated appeals. Constantine, however, did not understand the intensity of the Donatists' distaste for Caecilian. Consequently, when he tried to unite both groups under Caecilian's leadership, he had no chance of success. Large sums of money, the threat of persecution, and even persecution itself would not move the Donatists to accept Bishop Caecilian as the leader of the Catholic Church in Carthage, the seat once held by the beloved Cyprian. On the other hand, we must appreciate Constantine's sincere desire to maintain religious unity, which he believed would help keep the empire stable. As with emperors before him, the prayers and support of a unified religious community, now the Christians, were very important to him. Because of this mindset, he had to choose between competing groups; but why did he choose Caecilian's faction? Constantine's choice was probably made on practical as well as religious grounds. As Drake suggests,

> no greater contrast could be made with the actions of the party Constantine chose: the group now calling themselves "Catholics," while itself reflecting a variety of attitudes towards the state and non-Christian society, was nevertheless far more prepared to work with the existing power structure than were the Donatists.[40]

Drake argues that the Donatists represented a fault line that had developed because of Christianity's success: with Christianity now in favor with the worldly power, should Christians now soften or even renounce opposition to the powers of this world or should they hold fast in resisting the lure of the world and its power? While their Catholic opponents were willing to side with the emperor who had shown them favor, the Donatists opted for resistance even to the point of martyrdom; and by 317 they got the chance to prove their determination, for Constantine was determined to have unity, even if it meant using force. In spring of 317 he issued an edict allowing for the confiscation of Donatist churches and the exile of various leaders. Moreover, in a letter to Bishop Caecilian

---

40. Drake, *Constantine*, 230.

Constantine gave the bishop the authority to use secular power to enforce unity under the Roman bishop's rule.[41] When Donatus refused to surrender the churches under his rule, several Donatists were killed, and in one case, possibly at the *Basilica Maiorum*, the entire congregation was massacred.[42] In a sermon that may be from Bishop Donatus himself, we have a gruesome account of what took place. After informing his listeners that Caecilian was responsible[43] for this terrible massacre, he reports:

> While the tribune had prepared to indulge the wishes of the traitors and an abundance of blood had cooled the heat of their cruelty, some of the brethren entered the basilica again for however much time they could and held funerals for the martyrs. What passion of soul! What groans of lamentation! What devotion! Dashing among the bodies of the massacred, they hurried to identify each of those lying there. When children happened on the bodies of their parents cast upon the ground, and parents on the bodies of their children, you could see some of them holding their dead in their arms. Other half-dead themselves sank down in grief at the unexpected sight.[44]

Yet even this massacre did not stop the Donatists, but, according to Tilley, "merely succeeded in creating heroic Donatist martyrs instead of subservient new Catholics."[45] Emperor Constantine soon realized he could not bring unity to the African church by force. On May 5, 321 he granted toleration to the Donatists:

> But since our policy was not able to tame that power of ingrained wickedness, deep-seated though it be only in a few minds, and

41. Eusebius, *Hist. eccl* 10.6. At the end of the letter, Constantine says, "Wherefore, if thou seest any of these men persevering in this madness, thou shalt, without any hesitancy, proceed to the aforesaid judges, and report it to them, that they may animadvert upon them, as I commanded them, when present. May the power of the great God preserve thee many years."

42. Frend, *Donatist*, 160.

43. Tilley, *Stories*, 58.

44. PL 8:757: "Interea cum traditorum votis tribunus obsequi paravisset, cumque ardorem saevitiae saguinis copia satiasset, basilicam rursus aliqui fratres ingressi qualia pro tempore poterant obsequia martyribus exhibebant. Quae tunc animorum perturbatio! qui profluvii lacrymarum! qui lamentationum gemitus! quae inter cadavera trucidatorum discurrens pietas uniuscuiusque iacentis faciem dignoscere properavit! Ubi cum filii parentum, filiorum parentes prostrata corpora reperirent, videres alios suorum amplexibus inhaerentes, alios repentino visu percussos consedisse semianimes."

45. Tilley, *Stories*, xvi.

in this depravity they continued to plead on their own behalf, so as in no way to allow the object of their criminal delight to be wrested from them, we must take measures, while this whole business concerns but a few, that the mercy of Almighty God towards his people should be temperately applied. For we ought to expect the remedy from him to whom all good prayers and deeds are dedicated.[46]

Several times in this edict, Constantine claims that the persons causing the trouble are "but a few," but this was far from the truth. The Donatist numbers were strong throughout North Africa, but especially in the Numidian countryside. Moreover, after 321 they continued to grow, outpacing their Catholic opponents. It is also important to note that Constantine may have had other reasons for showing toleration to the Donatists. By 321 he was preparing for war with Licinius and, according to Gaddis, "part of Constantine's strategy was to paint his former ally as a persecutor in order to win the sympathies of Christians in the east, and the last thing he needed was to attract the same label upon himself."[47]

WHERE IS THE AFRICAN CHURCH:
WITH THE DONATISTS OR PARS MACARII?

From the initial outbreak of the controversy in 311 until 346, the Donatist Church was the majority church in North Africa. Despite imperial rulings against it, the Donatist Church continued to thrive during this period, especially in Numidia. The Donatists also expanded their territory by sending a bishop to head an existing congregation in Rome and founding a church in Spain.[48] Perhaps because of this success, when his rival died in 346, Bishop Donatus requested that Emperor Constans recognize him as the senior bishop of Carthage. At the Council at Arles in 314, Bishop Miltiades had stipulated that when there were two bishops in a town, one Catholic and one Donatist, the senior bishop, whether Catholic or Donatist, would be recognized as the primate or head of the Church in that locale. Consequently, when Bishop Donatus' rival died, Donatus became in fact the senior bishop in Carthage and therefore requested to

---

46. Optatus, *Against the Donatists* (tr. Edwards), Appendix 9, 196.

47. Gaddis, *No Crime*, 58.

48. Tilley, *Bible*, 69.

be recognized as such.[49] But this request proved to be a terrible mistake. On the advice of his religious adviser Bishop Hosius, Emperor Constans sent two imperial notaries, Paul and Macarius, with troops to investigate the situation. The imperial agents were not at all sympathetic to the Donatist cause and therefore were intent on enforcing an edict of unity under Catholic leadership.[50] On arrival Paul and Macarius attended the church services of Caecilian's successor, Bishop Gratus, and spoke openly on behalf of the Catholics. Seeing this hypocrisy, Donatus refused to meet with the emperor's agents or to accept any money from them and told his clergy to do likewise.[51] Because Bishop Donatus had seen how Emperor Constantine and now his son Constans had favored the party of Caecilian, he replied, "What has the church to do with the emperor"?[52] In addition, news of this mistreatment reached Numidia, and Donatists in that region were moved to resistance. As Paul and Macarius approached Numidia, between Theveste and Thamugadi, the populace became increasingly hostile. When the officials arrived in Numidia, Bishop Donatus of Bagai called on the Circumcellions[53] from the surrounding areas, withdrew to a fortified storehouse-basilica, and resisted the imperial authorities.[54] Paul and Macarius suppressed the rebellion. In the aftermath, Bishop Donatus of Bagai and the other rebels were killed.[55] According to Optatus, the Donatists were to blame for this massacre because they injured a few soldiers, who in turn became so infuriated that even their captain could not stop them from shedding blood. Thus, Optatus argues, the Catholics could not be held responsible for the slaughter.[56]

Despite the violence inflicted on them, the Donatists held a meeting after this incident and decided to send a few elder bishops to try to reason with the imperial agents. On June 29, 347, they held a meeting with Paul and Macarius at the agents' headquarters in Vegesel (Ksar el Kelb). The

49. Tilley, *Stories,* xxv.

50. Tilley, *Bible,* 70.

51. Frend, *Donatist,* 178.

52. Optatus, *Schis.* 3.3.

53. The Circumcellions were a militant branch of the Donatist Church. They offered the church militant resistance to repression but also caused it embarrassment by their outlandish behavior.

54. Optatus, *Schis.* 3.4.

55. Bishop Donatus of Bagai was killed, not Bishop Donatus of Carthage.

56. Optatus, *Schis.* 3.4.

meeting did not go well. After the Donatist bishop Marculus criticized
the actions of the imperial agents, Macarius became so enraged that he
had the bishops bound to pillars and flogged like criminals.[57] He then had
Bishop Marculus paraded around the surrounding area of Numidia before sending him to prison. After a few days, in the dead of night, soldiers
took him from prison and had him thrown from a cliff. Apparently they
chose this method of doing away with him expecting that his body would
either not be found or be so mangled that it could not be identified—or
that, even if his body was found and identified, it could be claimed that he
threw himself off the cliff, for Catholics at the time were spreading rumors
that Donatists sought to martyr themselves in various ways, including
throwing themselves down from heights. The Donatist account, however,
claims not only that Bishop Marculus was given a vision by God before
his demise informing him that he would be a blessed martyr for Christ
but also that his body was not mangled from the fall and was discovered
only by a miracle from God:

> Because their search could not be successful without the Lord,
> lightning was sent to that place to reveal the location which they
> were all seeking. The radiance of the cloud served as an indicator
> to point out the body longed for by the brethren. On that spot
> what weeping mixed with all their joy! What embraces round his
> distinguished limbs! At last when with difficulty they were all sat-
> isfied, funeral rites were celebrated with great joy by the brethren
> and the honor of a religious burial was restored with the greatest
> jubilation. For the glory of his name, the Lord revealed everything
> that the enemy tried to conceal. O the memorable and extraordi-
> nary martyrdom of blessed Marculus! O the example of unshaken
> virtue eagerly sought by all the devout![58]

Bishop Marculus thus became a martyr, a hero, and an example for other
Donatists to follow.

57. Frend, *Donatist*, 179.

58. PL 8:766: "Quia et hoc sine Domino esse non poterat, desideratum ab omnibus
locum quae ad hoc missa fuerant fulgura prodiderunt, et exoptatum fratribus corpus
index nubis candor ostendit. Qui tunc illic fuit omnium mixtus cum gaudiis fletus, qui
circa illustria membra complexus? Vix denique a cunctis satietate percepta, suprema
ingenti obsequia fratrum laetitia celebrata sunt, et religiosus supulturae honor cum
triumphis maximis restitutus est. Totum enim in gloriam nominis sui repraesentaverat
Dominus, quidquid fraudare tentaverat inimicus, O memorabile beati Marculi atque
insigne martyrium! o appetendum devotis omnibus inincussae virtutis exemplum!"
(Translation from Tilley, *Stories*, 87).

The Donatists continued to have opportunities for martyrdom, for Emperor Constans went on trying to suppress the Donatist church in Numidia and Carthage, sending various leaders, including Bishop Donatus of Carthage, into exile. To make matters worse for the party of Donatus, on August 15, 347, an imperial decree proclaimed "unity between the two churches under the Catholic bishop Gratus."[59]

The imperial authorities not only sided with Caecilian's successor, but by force and imperial decree made his group the official Catholic Church. In response the Donatists rioted, but to no avail. Bishop Donatus, who was now exiled, was never to set foot in Africa again. Nonetheless, eventually Emperor Constans would understand something that his father came to acknowledge years before: that the sword cannot establish unity. Emperor Constans also realized that making martyrs was counterproductive, so he withdrew his troops from Africa and allowed both groups, Donatist and Catholic, the freedom of worship. He did not, however, recall Bishop Donatus or the other bishops sent into exile. As a result, during the next period of Christianity in North Africa (348-361) the Donatist movement declined, as many of its leaders were exiled or in hiding as a result of the initial suppression by Constans. According to Frend, during the corresponding period the Catholics were not able to exploit their victory, for many of the Catholic clergy were corrupt. Consequently, very few Donatists were persuaded to join the Catholic Church in Africa. Moreover, Frend maintains that the *tempora Macariani* left as deep a mark on the Donatist Numidians as did the great persecution on the Christian community as a whole.[60] Future Donatist leaders would never allow the Catholics to forget their involvement in persecuting their Church; and from this point on, the Donatists would refer to the Catholic Church as *pars Macarii*—the "party of Macarius"—and to Catholics as *Macariani*.[61] This designation was not without some justification, for right after the persecution of 347 the Catholic bishop Gratus held a council (348/349) and called Paul and Macarius, the persecutors of the Donatists, "'holy servants of God sent by the emperor Constans to end the schism of our church."[62] Here, Bishop Gratus clearly identified

---

59. Frend, *Donatist*, 179.

60. Ibid., 185.

61. Ibid., 188.

62. PL 8:774: "Gratias Deo omnipotenti et Christo Jesu . . . qui imperavit religiosissimo Constanti imperatori, ut votum gereret unitatis, et mitteret ministros sancti operis famulos Dei Paulum et Macarium."

the success of his church with the state and praised the emperor for his involvement. Future Donatist leaders would spare no effort in condemning the Catholics as persecutors of the true church. In their view, it was unpardonable for Christians to join forces with the government in persecuting fellow Christians. From the Donatist perspective, this was unmistakable proof that their Catholic opponents, now likened to "gentiles" and labeled "the party of Macarius," had placed themselves in opposition to the true church.

7

From Julian to Augustine

EMPEROR JULIAN AND THE DONATIST REVIVAL

The reign of Emperor Julian (361–363) was short, but it helped bring about a revival of the Donatist Church. As Julian began recalling persons who had been banished during Constans' reign, the Donatist bishops Pontius and Macrobius of Rome pleaded their case, asking that they too be allowed to return to Africa.[1] Julian not only granted this request but also ordered that the Donatist church buildings and other property seized by the Catholics in 347 be restored. Even though Julian's reign lasted less than two years, this brief period allowed the Donatists to reestablish themselves throughout North Africa. This set the stage for the long and successful episcopate of Bishop Parmenian of Carthage.

When the Donatists began returning in 361, they must have been filled with pent-up anger toward their Catholic rivals. Moreover, in the tradition of Cyprian, they used various Old Testament scriptures regarding the Levitical priesthood as justification for avoiding anything their Catholic rivals had touched.[2] Thus, as Frend narrates,

> the altars at which they had worshipped only a short time before
> were broken up and burnt, the communion wine thrown to the
> dogs or heated into a powerful stimulant and drunk. The Catholic
> liturgical vessels were thrown out of windows to be smashed and
> their fragments sold off at the fairs for what they could fetch.
> Those who hesitated to participate were taunted with adhering to
> the "Macarians" and accused of "idolatry." The Donatist leaders

1. Optatus, *Schis.* 2.16. According to Optatus, Emperor Julian did this to disturb the peace between the two groups.

2. One scripture used by Cyprian is Lev. 21:21: "No man that hath a stain or a blemish shall come nigh to offer gifts to the Lord." Cyprian, *Ep.* 73.

saw in such events a just retribution and a necessary purge. As
Parmenian pointed out in 363/4, "Those things which had been
touched by the defiled were themselves defiled and should thus
be destroyed."[3]

However, according to Bishop Optatus (who may have been an eye-
witness to some of these events), the very dogs to which the Donatists
fed the eucharistic meal became mad and turned on their masters and bit
them. Optatus saw this as divine justice.[4] The feud between the two parties
was at times tragic and at times comical. The more radical Donatists, however, according to Optatus, went beyond mere purging of things to violence against human beings. When Bishops Felix of Zabi and Januarius of
Flumen Piscium met resistance to an attack trying to take over a Catholic
church (presumably one previously held by the Donatists) in the town
of Lemellefense (Kherbet Zembian), the two clerics had men climb onto
the roof of the church to throw roof tiles at the inhabitants below, killing
the deacons Primus and Donatus and wounding several other Catholics.[5]
These two men are noted in the Roman record of martyrs.[6] Optatus also
reports the mistreatment of Catholic virgins and other atrocities by the
Donatists. Throughout the controversy both sides perpetrated violence;
but now the Donatists, like their Catholic opponents in times past, were
emboldened by the support of secular powers; and what Optatus and his
group saw as the work of the devil, the Donatists saw as the justice of
God. Optatus is careful to point out every Donatist atrocity, but he does
not assign any blame to Macarius and the Catholics for the persecution
of the Donatists in 347; nor does Optatus show any appreciation for how
the Donatists may have felt when their churches were confiscated by force
in 347 and how in 361 they may thus felt justified in their anger when affairs finally swung in their favor. Neither the Donatists nor their Catholic
rivals were willing to admit to any wrongdoing by their own side. As a
result, peaceful reconciliation ultimately became impossible.

Nonetheless, as the Donatists continued to make gains throughout
North Africa and became the majority church in that region, they did

3. Frend, *Donatist*, 189.

4. Optatus, *Schis.* 2.19.

5. Ibid., 2.18. According to Optatus (2.17–19), there were other murders commited
by the Donatists, but some of his accounts may be exaggerated.

6. Willis, *Augustine*, 17. According to Frend, this event probably happened in 363.
Frend, *Donatist*, 189.

not openly persecute their Catholic opponents. During Parmenian's reign and into the early period of Augustine's priesthood (391-5), Augustine himself reports that the Donatists did not oppress their Catholic neighbors in northern Numidia and that religious questions could be discussed in relative calm.[7] Moreover, Catholic councils were able to meet in places where the Donatists were the majority. Frend correctly notes that the Catholics were always ready to claim toleration for themselves when they were in a minority, but a decade later, when the tables turned, they were not willing to grant the same to the Donatists.[8]

By the time of Bishop Parmenian not only were the Donatists the majority church, but they were recognized as the legitimate Catholic Church of the African provinces by various churches in Asia minor.[9] Moreover, even after the death of Emperor Julian on June 26, 363, Bishop Parmenian continued to promote the Donatist cause. The Donatists owed much of their success to Parmenian's leadership skills and his gifted speaking ability, but other factors also helped push the movement forward during this period. Among these were the support that Parmenian had from various local officials. For example, after Julian's death, his successors Valentinian and Valens issued a law against the rebaptism of Catholics, but African provincial officials for the most part did not enforce this law, and apart from the brutal persecutions of Count Romanus, Parmenian had various local officials supporting him throughout his reign.[10] Emperor Valentinian was not interested in getting caught up in the affairs of the church. Another factor favoring the Donatists' success was their practice of preaching in Punic, so that the native people of the towns and countryside, who spoke little or no Latin, could understand their message and

7. Augustine's epistles 33, 34, 35, 43, and 44 testify to the amicable conditons between him and Donatist leaders.

8. Frend, *Donatist*, 213.

9. Tilley, *Bible*, 113–14. Concerning this period (337–363), Frend makes the following comment: "At this stage the Donatists were recruiting from all classes of the population. Despite the scandals which had accompanined the breach with Caecilian, many literate Africans regarded the Donatist Church as the true Catholic Church in Africa, and the successor of the church of Cyprian's time." Frend, *Donatist*, 170.

10. Julian supported the Donatists during his reign (361–363). From 372 to 375 the African Firmus, a supporter of the Donatists, led a successful rebellion against the Roman authorities. Flavian, the *comes* of Africa in 376/377 was a member of the Donatist church. Finally, Firmus' brother Gildo was in power as *comes* in 385. On Romanus, see Ammianus Marcellinus 29.5 and 9.1–2. Firmus claimed he was led to revolt against the Roman authorities because of Romanus' evil deeds.

be drawn into the Donatist fold.[11] Bishop Parmenian, moreover, wrote psalms in Punic that remained very popular among the Donatists even after Parmenian's death and helped to teach the illiterate.[12] Lastly, except for Bishop Optatus of Melevis, the Catholic bishops during this time were not men of distinction, and some of them were suspected of holding Arian views. For example, Bishop Restitutus' support of the Council of Ariminium brought the criticism of both Rome and Alexandria; in 378 Bishop Damasus of Rome summoned him to the former imperial capital to give an account of his heretical views.[13] It is also believed that Bishop Athanasius directed his work *Ad Afros* to influence Bishop Restitutus and other African bishops (Libyans and Egyptians) to reject the Council of Ariminium.[14] After Bishop Restitutus' tenure ended, Bishop Genethlius was elected as his successor. He was a gentle and peaceful bishop who went out of his way to prevent confrontations with his Donatist rivals. Moreover, according to Augustine, Bishop Genethlius brought about a certain amount of respect between the two groups when he used his influence to prevent the persecution of Donatists in his diocese. As a result, for a brief period, both groups worshipped freely and developed genuine respect for one another.[15] All these factors enabled Bishop Parmenian, despite sporadic persecution and a few schisms within his ranks, to reign successfully as leader of the Donatist Church in North Africa.

11. Augustine, *Ep.*84. In this letter, Augustine refuses to send deacon Lucillus back to Sitifis because in that territory there were Catholic preachers able to preach in Punic, but in Hippo there was a shortage of such men. This sagacious move by Augustine helped the Catholics gain ground after he became bishop.

12. Augustine, *Ep.* 55.34. One of the first things Augustine did when he became a priest was to write a psalm in imitation of Parmenian: *Psalmus contra partem Donati.*

13. Frend, *Donatist*, 200.

14. Athanasius was critical of the Council of Ariminium because its leaders wrote a new creed that Athanasius believed devalued the creed of Nicea, so he and other Nicene bishops rejected it. In addition, several bishops at the council refused to condemn Arianism.

15. Augustine, *Ep.* 44.5.11. When Augustine was debating Fortunius he scored a point when he cornered the bishop into admitting that Bishop Genethlius was a good Christian. Once he did this, Augustine then asked him if he would rebaptize Genethlius. Fortunius could only admit that it was the Donatists' custom to baptize any Catholic that came to them, but he could not say anything negative against a man whom he witnessed showing Christian love to his rivals.

PARMENIAN: WHERE IS THE CHURCH IN NORTH AFRICA?
THE SACRAMENT OF BAPTISM AND THE TRUE CHURCH

One of Parmenian's most important accomplishments was his teaching on ecclesiology. In defense of the Donatists as the true representatives of Christianity in Africa, Parmenian wrote a work in five books, probably entitled *Adversus Ecclesiam Traditorum* (*Against the Church of the Traditores*[16]). Like much of the Donatist literature, his writings have not survived, but enough fragments have been quoted by Optatus of Milevis and Augustine of Hippo to give us an idea of his ecclesiology. With remarkable creativity, he depicts the nature of the church to show why the Catholics are not members of it. Using the symbolism of the church as the bride of Christ, Parmenian speaks of the church as having six endowments (*dotes*): 1) the *cathedra*, representing the authority and unity of the episcopacy; 2) the *angelus*, a rightly consecrated bishop or the guardian angels of the churches like those in Revelation; 3) the Spirit; 4) the *fons* or source of true baptism; 5) the *sigillum* or seal; and 6) the *umbilicus*, a properly consecrated altar.[17] Parmenian claims that the African Catholics not only did not possess these gifts (*dotes*) but also proved themselves to be false Christians by both betraying the word of God to pagan magistrates and calling in the secular powers to persecute the true church.[18] As Cyprian stated in *De unitate*, no one can think that he is a member of the church when he bears arms against the church and acts in opposition to God's institution.[19]

Although Parmenian maintains that the Donatist Church possessed the gifts of the true church, he nevertheless admits to problems that he must address. For one, the Donatist Church, in growing to become the majority church in Africa, had all sorts of members, and "there could be no pretense of being the minority church of the poor or the martyrs or exclusively that of the holy."[20] As the church of the majority, the Donatist Church had sinners, so that Parmenian has to recognize that

16. The word *traditor*, from which comes the English "traitor," means literally "one who hands over." It was virtually a technical term in the early church for those bishops and other church leaders who on demand from the authorities "handed over" the sacred books, especially the Bible.

17. Tilley, "Separatist," 263; Optatus, *Schis.* 2.2.

18. Frend, *Donatist*, 194.

19. Cyprian, *Unit. eccl*, 17.

20. Tilley, "Separatist," 262.

fact and develop an ecclesiology that can still justify separation from his Catholic rivals. Hence, he expands upon Donatist theology as it related to baptism, teaching that the baptismal font cannot be opened unless a church possesses the *dotes* or distinguishing gifts that God gave only to the true church. Naturally, Parmenian insists that his Catholic rivals did not possess these endowments, but, more importantly, he taught that during baptism there is an *ecclesiae supplet* that is present even when the priest is a sinner.[21] In this way the Holy Spirit still cleanses the baptizand and sanctifies the baptismal sacrament. Here Parmenian makes a useful distinction between the individual bishop and the church as an institution. On this point, Gordon Lewis offers an insightful assessment of the Donatist dilemma. The Donatists could not possibly examine the history of every Catholic bishop to see who had the taint of treason. It was simpler to excommunicate all their Catholic rivals and any other church that remained in fellowship with them.[22] And once this was done, Parmenian could claim that his church was holy because of its gifts. Tilley summarizes Parmenian's position:

> Thus, if a holy person in communion with the Donatist church (no matter how tenuously) administered a sacrament, well and good; it was a true sacrament because the minister was a member of the true church. If a sinful minister of the Donatist church administered a sacrament, there was no problem. The *dotes* of the church, not the spiritual gifts of the individual member, were the requirements.[23]

Thus Bishop Parmenian could insist that the true church in North African was the Donatist while admitting to the presence of sinners, albeit unknown sinners, among its clergy.

Being the majority church in North Africa, the Donatist Church had a diverse membership, which at times led to schisms and eventual separation from the Donatist body. For example, in 364, when the persecution of the Donatists increased, some bishops called on the Circumcellions for assistance. This action, however, alienated the more conservative Donatists who were embarrassed by the violent behavior of the Circumcellions. As a result, Bishop Rogatus of Cartenna and nine other persons started

21. Ibid., 263.
22. Lewis, "Violence," 107–8.
23. Tilley, "Separatist," 263.

their own church in that year. They continued as an independent body until 420. In addition to the Rogatist schism, there was a new generation of Donatists who had not experienced the persecution of Macarius and therefore were open to new and fresh ideas. One such person was the Donatist layman, Tyconius.

WHERE IS THE AFRICAN CHURCH?
PARMENIAN, TYCONIUS, AND AUGUSTINE

Tyconius was a profound thinker whose ideas influenced Augustine as well as Christians outside of Africa. No other Donatist could claim such influence on the bishop of Hippo, who used Tyconius' works as a foundation of his doctrine of grace and of his monumental work *De civitate Dei* (*On the City of God*).[24] Tyconius' view of the church, however, got him into trouble with Parmenian and other Donatist bishops. Tyconius taught among other things that

> the real division was not so much two churches as between two societies, each made up of individuals but governed by contrary wills, the one destined to salvation, the other to destruction. "Satan dwells everywhere: the throne of Satan is evil men." The distinction between the righteous and unrighteous was not predestined in individual cases: each could be a member of the *Civitas Dei* or the *Civitas Diaboli*. Penitence, contemplation, and consideration of eternity were possible for all and were the means by which grace was acquired and the means too of preparation for the first resurrection experienced in the sacrament of baptism. In the last resort it was penance, or the continuous striving to do God's will, which divided the true from the false Christians.[25]

Tyconius' teaching did not demand separation of the righteous from the unrighteous in this age. He held that the righteous would prevail in spite of any evil works by hypocrites or heretics and that separation between the true believers and the unrighteous would take place on the Last Day; at such time the African church would come into her own.[26] When Tyconius insisted that the separation of believers would be postponed until the Last Day instead of demanding separation from unrighteous

24. Willis, *Augustine*, 21.
25. Frend, *Donatist*, 204.
26. Ibid., 205.

persons, namely the African Catholics, now, Bishop Parmenian became critical of his teaching. When Parmenian could not persuade Tyconius to change his position, he summoned a council (circa 385) and had Tyconius excommunicated.[27] As Tilley notes, Parmenian was trying to provide the Donatist church with a new ecclesiology to suit changing circumstances, namely the reality of sinners within the true church.[28] As a result of his excommunication, Tyconius was unable to influence the Donatists away from Cyprian's reliance on the Levitical ideas of priestly purity as a model for the church toward a gospel view of the Church as containing both wheat and tares (Matt 13:24–29). Notwithstanding, Tyconius continued his writing, completing his *Commentary on the Apocalypse* (383), now lost, and a very popular work entitled *Liber regularum* (*Book of Rules*), which has survived almost intact.[29] Augustine incorporated the teaching of *Liber regularum* into his work *Teaching Christianity*.[30]

In writing after the death of Tyconius and Parmenian (circa 408), Augustine sought to exploit the division between the two to attack the Donatists, making two claims: first, that Tyconius was excommunicated because, in opposition to the Donatists, he taught that the true church was diffused throughout the whole world (and not only in North Africa among the Donatists); and second, that Tyconius taught that no one could be stained by the sin of another. Concerning the first point, Tilley notes that this is not a true representation either of what the Donatists taught or why Tyconius was excommunicated. The Donatist tradition did not deny the legitimacy of the church throughout the world. In fact, Bishop Parmenian was a product of one of those churches (probably that of Spain). Moreover, the Donatists did not claim that there were no valid churches outside of Africa but only that their Catholic rivals were not the true church in Africa. As Tilley correctly notes, these exclusivist claims covered only the area of North Africa.[31]

27. Ibid., 205. Frend states, "We know the facts only; of the background, nothing has survived."

28. Ibid., 205.

29. For a careful examination of Tyconius' *Liber Regularum*, see Bright, *Tyconius* and Tilley, *Bible*, 112–29.

30. Augustine sent a copy of Tyconius' work to Bishop Aurelius, asking if the bishop had read the work and what he thought of it. Augustine, *Ep.* 41.2.

31. Tilley, *Bible*, 113–14.

However, Augustine's second point, that Tyconius taught that no person could be stained by the sin of another, was in fact the deciding issue between Tyconius and his bishop. In his attempt to deal with a majority church (which obviously included sinners), he emphasized an individual's need for repentance. This was important, because he maintained that the division was not between two churches but between two societies of contrary wills. Thus the Christians' aim was not to avoid one another (as a contagion) but rather, above all else, to seek God's will and do penance when one sinned. A person was not contaminated by the sin of another. For this reason, Tyconius refused to label non-Donatist Christian churches as apostate and "more daringly for a Donatist, he refused to recognize the Donatist Church as the visible faithful remnant waiting the return of the Lord."[32] Thus, Tyconius' answer to the question "Where is the African church?" could have brought unity to the Christians of North Africa if the Donatists had been willing to listen to him. For Tyconius rejected rebaptism and the contamination of others as a reason to separate. Following the parable of the wheat and the tares in Matt 13:24–25, Tyconius believed the church contained both saints and sinners.

Augustine would use Tyconius' teachings in future debates with Donatist leaders.

DE BAPTISMO: AUGUSTINE'S REFUTATION OF THE DONATIST CLAIM TO CYPRIAN

Around 400 Augustine wrote a work on baptism in seven books, *De baptismo* (*On Baptism*), in which he attempted to refute both the Donatists' practice of rebaptism and their claim to Cyprian, their blessed martyr and hero. Because Augustine not only forcefully argues his own teaching on baptism but also records key positions of the Donatists, I will examine the first book of *De baptismo* very closely.[33] This will elucidate the Africans' understanding of baptism and show why each group believed itself to be the one true church in Africa. In the opening, Augustine declares:

> Wherefore in this treatise we have undertaken, with the help of God, not only to refute the objections which the Donatists have

32. Bright, *Tyconius*, 11.

33. I choose to focus on book one for two reasons: 1) in this book Augustine attempts to refute the Donatists' claim to Cyprian; and 2) this book outlines his basic arguments, which are repeated in the other six books.

been wont to urge against us in this matter, but also to advance
what God may enable us to say in respect of the authority of the
blessed martyr Saint Cyprian, which they endeavor to use as a
prop, to prevent their perversity from falling before the attacks of
truth. And this we propose to do, in order that all whose judgment
is not blinded by party spirit may understand that, so far from
Cyprian's authority being in their favor, it tends directly to their
refutation and discomfiture.[34]

Augustine thus endeavors to show that Cyprian's authority actually
refutes the Donatists' position. Interestingly, however, Augustine begins
his argument against the Donatists' practice of rebaptism by stressing
a point on which both parties agreed, stating: "no one of the Donatists
themselves denies that even apostates retain the grace of baptism; for
when they return within the pale of the church and are converted through
penance, it is never given to them a second time, and so it is ruled that it
never could have been lost."[35]

Here Augustine makes a point with which the Donatists could not
disagree, for the Donatists had allowed persons who had left their communion during the Maximianist schism to return later without the repetition of baptism. Augustine highlights this practice, for in it he believes he
has found the perfect argument to support his position allowing a valid
baptism to occur outside the church. He continues:

So those too who in the sacrilege of schism depart from the communion of the church certainly retain the grace of baptism, which
they received before their departure, seeing that, in case of their
return, it is not again conferred on them; whence it is proved that
what they had received while within the unity of the church, they
could not have lost in their separation. But if it can be retained
outside, why may it not also be given there? If you say, "It is rightly
given without the pale," we answer, "As it is not rightly retained,

---

34. Augustine, *Bapt.* 1.1.1: "Quapropter in hoc opere adiuvante Domino suscepimus
non solum ea refellere, quae de hac re nobis Donatistae obiectare consuerunt, sed etaim
de beatissimi martyris Cypriani auctoritate, unde suam perversitatem, ne veritatis im-
petu cadat, fulcire conantur, quae Dominus donaverit dicere, ut intellegant omnes, qui
non studio partium caecati indicant, non solum eos non adiuvari auctoritate Cypriani,
sed per ipsam maxime convinci atque subverti." Translation from King, NPNF 4.

35. *Bapt.* 1.1.2: "Nullus autem illorum negat habere baptismum etiam apostatas,
quibus utique redeuntibus et per paenitentiam conversis dum non redditur, amitti non
potuisse iudicatur."

and yet is in some sense retained, so it is not indeed rightly given, but yet it is given."[36]

Augustine insists that the fact that apostates leave the church for a period and then return without rebaptism demonstrates that baptism can occur outside the church. Augustine does not attempt to refute the Donatists by scripture but by the fact that rebaptism is not given to apostates or backsliders of either party. However, Augustine adds a crucial qualification to this argument: he insists that although baptism can occur outside the communion of the church, it is not fully profitable to individual Christians until they are reconciled to the unity of the church. So the key element that holds this teaching together for Augustine is unity: "But as, by reconciliation to unity, that begins to be profitably possessed which was possessed to no profit in exclusion from unity, so, by the same reconciliation, that begins to be profitable which without it was given to no profit."[37] His argument here is more creative than convincing. For Augustine appears to be saying that baptism which occurs outside the communion of the church is both valid and invalid, or that this baptism is only partially valid (as he says, possessed but to no profit) until one is reconciled to the unity of the church, at which time it becomes completely valid or profitable. This naturally raises the question—and Augustine will have to address this later—of how such a half-valid baptism can bring about the remission of sins or regeneration. Before Augustine addresses this concern, however, he sets out to refute the Donatist policy of disqualifying Catholic bishops whom they deem to be unfit. Again using the Maximianist schism and his concept of unity as a basis for his argument, Augustine maintains that clergy cannot lose their ability to administer the sacrament:

> For the sacrament of baptism is what the person possesses who is baptized; and the sacrament of conferring baptism is what he pos-

---

36. *Bapt.* 1.1.2: "Sic et illi, qui per sacrilegium schismatis ab ecclesiae communione discedunt, habent utique baptismum, quem priusquam discederent acceperant. Nam si et ipsi redeant, non eis iterum datur; unde ostenduntur illud, quod acceperant in unitate positi, non potuisse amittere separati. Quod si haberi foris potest, etiam dari cur non potest? Si dicis: 'Non recte foris datur,' respondemus: 'Sicut non recte foris habetur et tamen habetur, sic non recte foris datur, sed tamen datur.'"

37. *Bapt.* 1.1.2: "Sicut autem per unitatis reconciliationem incipit utiliter haberi quod extra unitatem inutiliter habebatur, sic per eandem reconciliationem incipit utile esse quod extra eam inutiliter datum est."

sesses who is ordained. And as the baptized person, if he departs from the unity of the church, does not thereby lose the sacrament of baptism, so also he who is ordained, if he depart from the unity of the church, does not lose the sacrament of conferring baptism. If therefore the baptism be acknowledged which he could not lose who severed himself from the unity of the church, that baptism must also be acknowledged which was administered by one who by his secession had not lost the sacrament of conferring baptism. For as those who return to the church, if they had been baptized before their secession, are not rebaptized, so those who return, having been ordained before their secession, are certainly not ordained again.[38]

To buttress this point, Augustine cites the Maximianist schism (again) and the Donatists' treatment of Bishop Felicianus:

For Felicianus, when he separated himself from them with Maximianus, was not held by the Donatists themselves to have lost either the sacrament of baptism or the sacrament of conferring baptism. For now he is a recognized member of their own body in company with those very men whom he baptized while he was separated from them in the schism of Maximianus.[39]

Because the Donatists received Felicianus back in their communion after a bitter separation without refusing to recognize his ordination, this inconsistency, in Augustine's view, refutes the Donatists' claim that Caecilian's sin tainted other Catholic bishops and thereby made them unfit ministers of the sacraments. Thus Augustine maintained both that baptism could occur outside the communion of the church and that a bishop who departed from the communion of the church and returned did not lose his ordination. However, Augustine's teaching that baptism could occur outside the church created an interesting dilemma for the

38. *Bapt.* 1.1.2: "Sacramentum enim baptismi est quod habet qui baptizatur, et sacramentum dandi baptismi est quod habet qui ordinatur. Sicut autem baptizatus, si ab unitate recesserit, sacramentum baptismi non amittit, sic etiam ordinatus, si ab unitate recesserit, sacramentum dandi baptismi non amittit. Sicut ergo acceptatur baptismus quem non potuit amittere qui ab unitate discesserat, sic acceptandus est baptismus, quem dedit ille qui sacramentum dandi cum discederet non amiserat. Nam sicut redeuntes, qui priusquam recederent baptizati sunt, non rebaptizantur, ita reduentes, qui priusquam recederent ordinati sunt, non utique rursus ordinantur."

39. *Bapt.* 1.1.2: "Nam neque sacramentum baptismi neque sacramentum dandi baptismi quando ab eis cum Maximiano discessit Felicianus amisit; nunc enim eum secum habent cum eis ipsis, quos cum foris esset in Maximiani schismate baptizavit."

bishop of Hippo. Because he had forcibly taught that baptism could occur outside the communion of the church, he had the challenge of trying to defend this position on the one hand while trying to undermine the Donatists' practice of baptism—which occurred outside the church—on the other. To accomplish this, Augustine again appealed to his argument of unity and to the concept that something might be possessed while not being possessed properly:

> There are two propositions, moreover, which we affirm—that baptism exists in the Catholic Church, and that in it alone can it be rightly received—both of which the Donatists deny. Likewise, there are two other propositions which we affirm— that baptism exists among the Donatists, but that with them its is not rightly received—of which they strenuously confirm the former, that baptism exists with them; but they are unwilling to allow the latter, that in their church it cannot be rightly received.[40]

Augustine does not have any convincing scriptural arguments here to support his teaching against the Donatists but simply insists that their baptism is not rightly received. On the basis of this assumption, Augustine declares that people should not get baptized in a church where they know that the baptism is not rightly received; they should "prefer what is certain to what is false or uncertain."[41] Augustine concludes that if a person knowingly prefers what is a false or at best an uncertain baptism to what is certain and true, then that person commits a grave sin. Moreover, if a person receives this baptism in ignorance, then that person also commits sin, albeit a lesser sin.[42] In the face of such criticism of the Donatists' baptismal sacrament, one is tempted to ask, as did the Donatists: how then can their baptism remit sins and bring about regeneration? Augustine, aware of this problem, offers the following defense:

> But they think within themselves that they show very subtlety in asking whether the baptism of Christ in the party of Donatus makes men sons or not; so that, if we allow that it does make them sons, they may assert that theirs is the church, the mother which

---

40. *Bapt.* 1.3.4 : "Duo sunt enim quae dicimus, et esse in catholica baptismum et illic tantum recte accipi; utrumque horum Donatistae negant. Item alia duo dicimus, esse apud Donatistas baptismum, non autem illic recte accipi; horum duorum illi unum magnopere adfirmant, id est esse ibi baptismum, non autem illic recte accipi nolunt fateri."

41. *Bapt.* 1.5.6: "Vero ergo falsis aut incertis certa praepone."

42. *Bapt.* 1.5.6.

could give birth to sons in the baptism of Christ; and since the church must be one, they may allege that ours is no church. But if we say that it does not make them sons, "Why then," say they, "do you not cause those who pass from us to you to be born again in baptism, after they have been baptized with us, if they are not thereby born as yet?"[43]

Augustine, by quoting the logic and argumentation used by the Donatists, actually exposes the weakness of his position. He admits that the Donatists believe that they have made a subtle point against him, but he will not acknowledge that they in fact have. Almost as if he is insulted by his opponents' logic, Augustine counters:

> Just as though their party gained the power of generation in virtue of what constitutes its division, and not from what causes its union with the churches. For it is severed from the bond of peace and charity, but it is joined in one baptism. And so there is one church which alone is called Catholic; and whenever it has anything of its own in these communions of different bodies which are separate from itself it is most certainly in virtue of this which is its own in each of them that it, not they, has the power of generation.[44]

Here, Augustine seems to acknowledge, if only reluctantly, that the Donatists' baptism had the ability to regenerate, although he will not say the baptism of the Donatists has generative power, but only that baptism itself has the power of generation. Augustine speaks here almost as if baptism existed in itself and apart from people, at least people in the Donatist Church. But he quickly cancels this modest acknowledgement by insisting that their baptism is invalid for another reason: it is not joined to the unity of the church:

---

43. *Bapt.* 1.10.13: "Sed videntur sibi argutissime quaerere, utrum generet filio baptismus Christi in parte Donati an non generet, ut si concesserimus quod generet suam esse adseverent ecclesiam matrem quae filios potuit de Christi baptismate generare, et quia unam oportet esse ecclesiam, ex hoc iam nostram non esse ecclesiam criminentur. Si autem dixerimus 'non generat,' 'Cur ergo,' inquiunt, 'apud vos non renascuntur per baptismum qui transeunt a nobis ad vos, cum apud nos fuerint baptizati, si nondum nati sunt?'"

44. *Bapt.* 1.10.14: "Quasi vero ex hoc generat unde separata est et non ex hoc unde coniuncta est. Separata est enim a vinculo caritatis et pacis, sed iuncta est in uno baptismate. Itaque una est ecclesia quae sola catholica nominatur, et quidquid suum habet in communionibus diversorum a sua unitate separatis, per hoc quod suum in eis habet ipsa utique generat, non illae."

The generation, then, in each case proceeds from the church, whose sacraments are retained, from which any such birth can alone in any case proceed, and though not all who receive its birth belong to its unity, which shall save those who persevere even to the end. Nor is it those only that do not belong to it who are openly guilty of the manifest sacrilege of schism, but also those, who, being outwardly joined to its unity, are yet separated by a life of sin. For the church had herself given birth to Simon Magus through the sacrament of baptism; and yet it was declared to him that he had no part in the inheritance of Christ.[45]

With this type of argumentation it is understandable why the Donatists referred to Augustine as a new Carneades.[46] For on one hand he admits if ever so reluctantly that the Donatists' baptism can bring regeneration while on the other he argues (using his concept of unity) that it is nonetheless defective. Specifically, Augustine argues that Donatist baptism brings about a new birth but that this new birth is immediately made void because those baptized by Donatists are not joined to the unity of the church. Moreover, to further discredit what he had to admit, Augustine compares the Donatists to the arch-heretic of the early church, Simon Magus. They receive the church's baptism, but like Simon Magus they

45. *Bapt.* 1.10.14: "Haec itaque in omnibus generat cuius sacramenta retinentur, unde possit tale aliquid ubicumque generari, quamvis non omnes quos generat ad eius pertineant unitatem, quae usque in finem perseverantes salvabit. Neque enim hi solum ad eam non pertinent qui separationis aperto sacrilegio manifesti sunt, sed etiam illi qui in eius unitate corporaliter mixti per vitam pessimam separantur. Etenim Simonem magum per baptisma ipsa pepererat, cui tamen dictum est quod non haberet partem in hereditate Christi."

46. Augustine thus records the charge made against him by the Donatist bishop Petilian: "He says that I slide in slippery places, but am held up, that I neither destroy nor confirm the objections that I make; that I devise uncertain things in the place of certainty; that I do not permit my readers to believe what is true, but cause them to look with increased suspicion on what is doubtful. He says that I have the accursed talents of the Academic philospher, Carneades." *C. litt. Petil.* 3.21.24. Carneades was a philosopher described thus by Lactantius in *Inst.* 15: "This Carneades, when he had been sent by the Athenians as ambassador to Rome, disputed copiously on the subject of justice, in the hearing of Galba and Cato, who had been censor, who was at that time the greatest of orators. But on the next day the same man overthrew his own argument by a disputation to the contrary effect, and took away the justice which he had praised on the preceding day, not indeed with the gravity of a philosopher, whose prudence ought to be firm and his opinion settled, but as it was by an oratorical king of exercise of disputing on both sides." Translation from ANF 7.

have no part in the inheritance of Christ because of their sin and so were reborn in vain.

The Donatists were well aware of the weakness of Augustine's logic and therefore challenged him either to admit or to deny that their baptism brought about the remission of sins. Augustine records this challenge:

> They ask also whether sins are remitted in baptism in the party of Donatus, so that, if we say that they are remitted, they may answer, then the Holy Spirit is there; for when by the breathing of our Lord the Holy Spirit was given to the disciples, He then went on to say, "Baptize all nations in the name of the Father, and of the Son, and of the Holy Spirit;" whosesoever sins ye remit, they are remitted unto them; and whosesoever sins ye retain, they then are retained." And if this is so, they say, then our communion is the church of Christ; for the Holy Spirit does not work the remission of sins except in the church. And if our communion is the church of Christ, then your communion is not the church of Christ. For that is one wherever it is, of which it is said, "My dove is but one; she is the only one of her mother;" nor can there be just so many churches as there are schisms. But if we should say that sins are not there remitted, then, say they, there is no true baptism; and therefore ought you to baptize those whom you receive from us. And since you do not do this, you confess that you are not in the church of Christ.[47]

Because the Donatists have skillfully exposed the weakness of Augustine's position, he is forced to admit or deny the remission of sins in the Donatists' baptismal sacrament:

> And so let them understand that men may be baptized in communions severed from the church, in which Christ's baptism is given and received in the said celebration of the sacrament, but that it will only then be of avail for the remission of sins when the

---

47. *Bapt.* 1.11.15: "Quaerunt etiam utrum peccata dimittantur per baptismum in parte Donati, ut si dixerimus dimitti respondeant: Ergo est illic Spiritus Sanctus, quia cum insufflante Domino datus esset discipulis, tunc secutus est et ait: 'Baptizate gentes in nomine Patris et Filii et Spiritus Sancti. Si cui dimiseritis peccata dimittentur ei, si cui tenueritis tenebuntur.' Et si ita est, inquiunt, communio nostra est ecclesia Christi; non enim praeter ecclesiam dimissionem peccatorum Spiritus Sanctus operatur. Et si nostra communio est ecclesia Christi, non est ecclesia Christi vestra communio. Una est enim, quaecumque illa sit de qua dictum est: 'Una est columba mea, una est matri suae,' nec possunt ecclesiae tot esse quot schismata. Si autem dixerimus non ibi dimitti peccata, ergo, inquiunt, non est illic verus baptismus, et propterea quos a nobis suscipitis vos baptizare debetis. quod quia non facitis, in ecclesia Christi vos non esse fatemini."

recipient, being reconciled to the unity of the church, is purged from the sacrilege of deceit, by which his sins were retained, and their remission prevented.[48]

I suggest the Donatists succeeded here in forcing Augustine to admit what he truly believed: that the baptism of the Donatists was not valid, for it did not remit sins until one was joined to the unity of the church, that is, the church to which Augustine belonged.[49]

After Augustine believes he has refuted the Donatists' teaching on baptism while upholding his teaching on the reality of baptism occurring outside the communion of the church, he concludes his first book by attempting to refute the Donatists' claim to Cyprian. Again, he uses his themes of unity and charity as the basis of his argument. Augustine knew that the Donatists followed the teaching of Cyprian on rebaptism, but he nevertheless insisted that they were not the martyr bishop's disciples. In fact, in a statement which undoubtedly would have been very offensive to the Donatists, Augustine asserts that because of Cyprian's charity and love of unity the bishop of Carthage could be forgiven for his wrong teaching on rebaptism:

> As it is written "For charity shall cover a multitude of sins." For, seeing that its absence causes the presence of all other things to be of no avail, we may well suppose that in its presence there is found pardon for the absence of some missing things. There are great proofs of this existing on the part of the blessed martyr Cyprian, in his letters—to come at last to him of whose authority they carnally flatter themselves are possessed, whilst by his love they are spiritually overthrown.[50]

Augustine's argument here is curious. Earlier in book one he acknowledged that Cyprian and the African fathers at the council in 256 taught rebaptism, but he nonetheless will not acknowledge that the Donatists

48. *Bapt.* 1.12.18: "Atque ita intelligant in communionibus ab ecclesia separatis posse homines baptizari, ubi Christi baptismus eadem sacramenti celebratione datur et sumitur, qui tamen tunc prosit ad remissionem peccatorum, cum quisque reconciliatus unitati sacrilegio dissensionis exuitur, quo eius peccata tenebantur et dimitti non sinebantur."

49. Augustine makes this point even more forcibly in *Bapt.* 4.2.2.

50. *Bapt.* 1.18.27–28: "Sicut scriptum est: 'quia caritas cooperit multitudinem peccatorum.' Qua enim absente cetera inaniter habentur, eadem praesente quaedam venialiter non habentur. Extant beati maytyris Cypriani in eius litteris magna documenta, ut ad illum iam veniam de cuius sibi auctoritate isti carnaliter blandiuntur, cum eius caritate spiritaliter perimantur."

have a right to claim Cyprian's authority. In Augustine's view, Cyprian's authority lies in the fact that he sought unity and love with Christians with whom he disagreed within the church. Thus, Augustine insists that the Donatists cannot claim his authority because "by his love they are spiritually overthrown." Moreover, Augustine continues to insist—as if Cyprian sought unity at all costs—that Cyprian would not separate from Christians with whom he disagreed:

> For when a bishop of so important a church, himself a man of so great merit and virtue, endowed with such excellence of heart and power of eloquence, entertained an opinion about baptism different from that which was to be confirmed by a more diligent searching into the truth; though many of his colleagues held what was not yet made manifest by authority, but was sanctioned by the past custom of the church, and afterwards embraced by the whole Catholic world; yet under these circumstances he did not sever himself, by refusal of communion from the others who thought differently, and indeed never ceased to urge on the others that they should "forbear one another in love, endeavoring to keep the unity of the Spirit in the bond of peace."[51]

Augustine is correct in citing Cyprian's desire for unity among a diversity of opinions, for Cyprian approved of and encouraged councils. However, Augustine misrepresented Cyprian's position by implying that Cyprian believed in unity at all cost or that he never ceased (*non destitit*) to forbear others in love and unity. Cyprian believed that every bishop shared in the "chair of Peter" and therefore had equal authority. However, as we have noted in his dispute with Stephen in chapter five, Cyprian chose the truth as outlined in scripture as he understood it above any tradition practiced within the church. Cyprian was first and foremost a bishop of Holy Scripture. He respected the opinions of other bishops because he believed in shared power among bishops. Nonetheless, when a bishop committed certain sins—lapsing in faith under persecution or admitting to communion persons who had not completed their penance,

---

51. *Bapt.* 1.18.28: "Cum enim tanti meriti, tantae ecclesiae, tanti pectoris, tanti oris, tantae virtutis episcopus aliud de baptismo arbitraretur quam erat diligentius inquisita veritas firmatura, multique eius collegae quamvis nondum liquido manifestatum id tamen tenerent, quod et praeterita ecclesiae consuetudo et postea totus catholicus orbis amplexus est, non se ille tamen a ceteris diversa sentientibus separata communione disiunxit et hoc etiam ceteris persuadere non destitit, ut sufferrent invicem in dilectione studentes servare unitatem Spiritus in vinculo pacis."

as happened in the Decian persecution—then Cyprian held an uncompromising position. Any lapsed clergy could remain in the church, but only after penance, the laying on of hands, and the renunciation of their ministry. In Cyprian's view, a clergyperson who had betrayed the church could not retain an office in the church. As noted in our earlier example of Basilides and Maretial, the Spanish bishops who had lapsed, Cyprian's idea of unity did not extend to maintaining communion with them when they refused to relinquish their office. In short, Augustine's suggestion that Cyprian would seek unity at all costs or that he "never ceased" to show love and unity is not true.[52] When Cyprian believed he was correct in rebaptizing heretics or in dismissing the lapsed Spanish bishops, he did not compromise his position to stay in unity with Stephen. In the latter case in particular, Cyprian did the exact opposite of what Augustine is suggesting here. Not only did Cyprian insist that the lapsed clergy of Spain resign, but he also told the people to separate from them—contrary to what Augustine repeatedly states. Cyprian believed, as did the Donatists later, that to remain in communion with such persons would be to make oneself a partaker of their sin. Thus, the Donatists were the rightful heirs of Cyprian. They knew his theology very well and followed him precisely on this point. When the Donatists maintained that the Catholics were stained by the sin of Caecilian, they separated themselves from the Catholics, and like Cyprian they would not be swayed from what they believed was the truth.

At the conclusion of book one of *De baptismo*, Augustine further suggests that Cyprian's desire for unity and love not only made up for his lack of insight into the baptismal sacrament but also made him a deserving candidate for martyrdom, at which time what was lacking in him was cleared away by his baptism in blood. Again, not shrinking from a statement that must have been very offensive to the Donatists, Augustine states:

> Whilst then that holy man entertained on the subject of baptism an opinion at variance with the true view, which was afterwards thoroughly examined and confirmed after most diligent consideration, his error was compensated by his remaining in catholic unity, and

52. Other places where Augustine emphasizes Cyprian's desire for unity: *Bapt.* 2.1.1, 2.3.4, 2.5.6, 2.6.7, 2.12, 2.8.13, 2.15.20, 3.2.2, 3.13.18, 4.12.19, 5.1.1. Sometimes Augustine acts as if his argument is made stronger by simply repeating it.

by the abundance of his charity; and finally it was cleared by the pruning-hook of martyrdom.[53]

Throughout book one, Augustine uses his concept of unity to refute both the Donatists' teaching on baptism and their claim to Cyprian. His arguments, however, would not have convinced a Donatist. As Evans suggests, Augustine at times writes as "if the Donatists were in fact Catholics who had to be persuaded on Catholic grounds not to rebaptize schismatics."[54] Moreover, for the most part, Augustine does not base his arguments in scripture but in the philosophy of his day. On this point, Frend correctly assesses the weakness in Augustine's approach:

> The distinction between "regular" and "valid" sacraments, of membership of the Church "visible" and "invisible," so clear to a modern or to a fourth-century student of Plotinus, was probably beyond the grasp of the native Berber; the simple metaphor used by Cyprian of the church as the ark—within the saved, outside the drowning multitude—conveyed the situation to them.[55]

While Augustine was wise to exploit the division between Tyconius and his Bishop Parmenian on the nature of the church, he was not as successful in disputing the Donatists' teaching on baptism and rebaptism and their claim to Cyprian's authority. As Evans notes, Augustine "shoots wide of the mark" in proving his claim. His arguments would certainly not have been convincing to Donatists, but maybe that is the point. Is Augustine addressing Catholics, speaking out of fear that they might leave the church and join the Donatist ranks? Evans believes this was a real possibility:

> Is one to suppose that an important reason why Catholics went over to the Donatists was precisely the latter's continuance of the African practice of rebaptism; that Augustine in this work really has this problem in mind; and that his grief over the defection of Catholics for this reason is in fact the ground of his repeatedly expressed horror of Donatist rebaptism? Probably.[56]

---

53. *Bapt.* 1.18.28: "Quod ergo ille vir sanctus de baptismo aliter sentiens quam se res habebat, quae postea pertractata et diligentissima consideratione firmata est, in catholica unitate permansit, et caritatis ubertate compensatum est et passionis falce purgatum."

54. Evans, *One and Holy*, 76.

55. Frend, *Donatist*, 205.

56. Evans, *One and Holy*, 77.

In summary, even though Augustine and the Donatists were speaking in different tongues, they were, in many ways, claiming the same thing. Both groups believed that their church was the true Catholic Church and that their opponents were schismatics or heretics. In addition, both groups insisted that the baptismal sacrament of their opponent was invalid. The Donatists insisted that the African Catholics' baptism was useless and therefore openly rebaptized them. Augustine, on the other hand, did not practice rebaptism, but taught that the Donatists' baptism was invalid until they joined the church to which he belonged. Thus, both groups claimed to be the true church in Africa, both groups claimed that their church was the place where the true sacraments were administered, and both groups—unfortunately—were equally adamant about these claims.

Within a few years after Augustine had completed his seven books against the Donatists' teaching on baptism (*De baptismo*), he wrote a three-book work against the Donatists' view of baptism in answer to the Donatist bishop Petilian. We shall examine this work in our next chapter.

8

Baptism, Persecution, and Resistance

BISHOP OPTATUS OF THAMUGADI AND COUNT GILDO

DURING THE PERIOD 368–398, immediately preceding the episcopate of Petilian, certain actions of the Donatists prompted an attempt by imperial authorities to suppress the movement. Many Donatists at this time were led by the revolutionary Bishop Optatus of Thamugadi.[1] The Circumcellions had become a military force that employed swords, spears, and other weapons to enforce whatever Bishop Optatus demanded. According to Augustine, Bishop Optatus was able to redistribute land, settle marriage disputes, evict unpopular heirs, and punish oppressive landowners by forcing them to abandon their estates. Donatists were at their peak during this period, for not only were they the majority church in south Numidia, but, according to Frend, they were gaining in Roman cities such as Constantine, Hippo, Rusiccade, and Calana, as they acquired a "quasi official standing in North Africa."[2] Count Gildo, who had been loyal to Emperor Theodosius when his brother Firmus had revolted years earlier, was beginning to dream of having Africa under his control. Tilley notes that after Theodosius' death in 395, Gildo "seemed to have neither respect for nor fear of the emperor's young sons Honorius and Arcadius."[3] Thus, in 397 Gildo held back the corn fleet from Rome and as a result was declared a public enemy by the Roman Senate. Meanwhile, Bishop Optatus had merged his religious power with Gildo's political rebellion. This proved fatal when Stilicho, in a surprise attack, defeated Gildo's army without much resistance. Gildo and Bishop Optatus were executed, and

1. Augustine, *Ep.* 43. 24.
2. Frend, *Donatist*, 210.
3. Tilley, *Bible*, 132.

the Donatists were clearly on the defensive and in need of a bishop who could rally their cause.

PETILIAN'S PASTORAL LETTER:
AN ATTEMPT TO RALLY HIS CHURCH

In 399, the Donatist bishop Petilian wrote a pastoral letter, *Epistula ad presbyteros et diaconos,* to rally the people within his church after the death of Bishop Optatus.[4] The three-book work of Augustine *Contra litteras Petiliani* contains this letter together with the initial disputes between him and Petilian.

When Petilian distributed his letter to the leaders and lay persons of the Donatist Church, it immediately caused a stir between Donatists and Catholics throughout North Africa. The Catholic bishop Fortunatus, Petilian's rival in Constantine, brought a copy of this letter to Augustine and requested that he respond to it immediately. According to Augustine, Petilian's reputation as an intelligent and eloquent speaker seemed to the bishop of Hippo in such disharmony with the quality of the letter that Augustine doubted the Donatist's authorship of it, even though one of Augustine's bishops had already verified its authenticity:

> I was unwilling to believe that it could be the letter of a man who, if fame speaks truly, is especially conspicuous among them for learning and eloquence. But some of those who were present when I read it, being acquainted with the polish and embellishment of his composition, gradually persuaded me that it was undoubtedly his address. I thought, however, that whoever the author might be, it required refutation, lest the writer should seem to himself, in the company of the inexperienced, to have written something of weight against the Catholic Church.[5]

---

4. Monceaux takes this title from Petilian's opening address as quoted by Augustine in *Petil.* 1.2: "Petilianus episcopus dilectissimis fratribus, compresbyteris et diaconibus, ministris per diocesim nobiscum in sancto evangelio constitutis: gratia vobis et pax a Deo patre nostro et Domino Iesu Christo." Monceaux, *Histoire,* 5:311.

5. Augustine, *Petil.* 1.1: "ut nollem credere illius hominis esse litteras, quem solet fama praedicare quod inter eos doctrina atque facundia maxime excellat. Sed quia me legente aderant quidam, qui eius sermonis cultum ornatumque cognoscerent, mihi persuadere coeperunt omnino eius esse illud eloquium. Ego tamen, cuiuslibet esset, refellendum putavi, ne, quisquis ea scripsit, aliquid sibi apud imperitos adversus catholicam scripsisse videretur." Translation from King, NPNF 4, slightly modernized in places.

At the time, Augustine was working on his commentary on Genesis and his work on the Trinity and may have felt it a waste of time to respond.[6] Nonetheless, because of the urgent request of his friend Fortunatus and the letter's content, he immediately answered Petilian's letter, though he at first had only a small fraction of this work in his possession. Thus the first book of *Contra litteras Petiliani* covers only one fifth of Petilian's letter. After Augustine completed and circulated this first book, Petilian received a copy of it and immediately attacked Augustine in his *Epistula I ad Augustinum*.

In the meantime, before learning that Petilian had responded to his first refutation, Augustine received a complete copy of Petilian's letter. In the second book of *Contra litteras Petiliani*, written around 401, Augustine attempted a systematic refutation of Petilian's entire work. He duplicated Petilian's pastoral letter in full, but with his own commentary inserted throughout, pointing out to his readers that he did not change one word of Petilian's letter but sought to refute him sentence by sentence and point by point, aiming to give the impression of a face-to-face debate (2.1). After Augustine had completed this second book, he finally received Petilian's first letter against him, in response to which he wrote the third book of *Contra litteras Petiliani* refuting Petilian's attack, but not as systematically as in book two.[7]

As noted earlier, Donatists were on the defensive. Not only did they meet one of their most formidable opponents in Bishop Augustine of Hippo, but his friend and former student Fortunatus was causing problems for Petilian in his own diocese of Constantine. Both bishops, Petilian and Fortunatus, accused each other of adding bishops to their respective dioceses, and each bishop would return accusations blow for blow.[8] That Fortunatus brought this letter to Augustine speaks to its likely influence in Constantine, perhaps among the Catholics as well as Donatists. To many Donatists, Petilian's pastoral letter was like a new gospel, and they recited passages of the tract from memory.[9] It was not

6. In his *Retractationes*, Augustine makes the following comment regarding the letters of Petilian: "Before I had finished the books *On the Trinity* and the books *On the Literal Meaning of Genesis*, circumstances compelled me to reply to a letter of Petilian, a Donatist, which he had written against the Catholic Church." Translation from Bogan, 171.

7. Monceaux, *Histoire*, 6:8.

8. Monceaux, *Histoire*, 6:7–8.

9. Monceaux, *Histoire*, 6:35.

only a great success in the Donatist community but was also noticed by Catholics. By 400 Bishop Petilian had emerged as the leading representative of the Donatist Church, and it was this epistle that brought him into direct confrontation with the most persistent leader of the Catholic Church, Bishop Augustine of Hippo. To this exchange between formidable opponents I shall now turn.

PETILIAN: TRUE VERSUS FALSE BAPTISM

The contents of Petilian's letter make clear why Catholics were eager to have it refuted. Petilian did not spare words in attacking Augustine and the Catholics and depicting them in the worst light possible.[10]

Equally understandable is why Donatists regarded it as like a new gospel. Petilian presents Donatist theology with force and clarity, supported by a wealth of scriptures. The issues are not new, but Petilian adds his voice to the points of disagreement between the two churches, covering three main themes: 1) the true baptism of Donatists versus the false baptism of Catholics, 2) the Catholics' appeal to secular powers to persecute the true church, and 3) the Donatists' justification for separation from their Catholic rivals.[11] After his opening greetings, Petilian immediately launches into a defense of the Donatist baptism: "Those who have polluted their souls with a guilty laver, under the name of baptism, reproach us with baptizing twice—than whose obscenity, indeed, any kind of filth is more cleanly, seeing that through a perversion of cleanli-

---

10. Two examples of the harsh criticism Petilian leveled against Augustine are as follows. In *Petil.* 2.8–17: "We must consider, I say and declare, how far the treacherous *traditor* is to be accounted dead while yet alive. Judas was an apostle when he betrayed Christ; and the same man was already dead, having spiritually lost the office of an apostle, being destined afterwards to die by hanging himself, as it is written: '"I have sinned," says he, "in that I have betrayed the innocent blood"'; and he departed, and went and hanged himself." The *traditor* perished by the rope: he left the rope for others like himself, of whom the Lord Christ cried aloud to the Father, 'Father, those that Thou gavest me I have kept, and none of them is lost, but the son of perdition; that the Scripture might be fulfilled. For David of old had passed this sentence on him who was to betray Christ to the unbelievers: 'Let another take his office. Let his children be fatherless, and his wife a widow.'" *Petil.* 2.51–117: "If you wretched men claim for yourselves a seat, as we said before, you assuredly have the one of which the prophet and psalmist David speaks as being the seat of the scornful. For you it is rightly left, seeing that the holy cannot sit therein."

11. There is no set pattern, but throughout his letter Petilian repeats these three themes.

ness they have come to be made fouler by their washing."[12] Petilian here argues that, while Catholics accuse Donatists of baptizing twice, it is they, the Catholics, who have a baptism that is polluted (*sordes*), using water that has been contaminated (*inquinari*). Petilian's argument continues, "for when you in your guilt performed what is false, I do not celebrate baptism twice, which you have never celebrated once."[13] Here Petilian claims the Donatists were not baptizing persons twice, but rather baptizing them once in the true church. Following in the tradition of Cyprian, he maintained that valid baptism was rooted in a true church in which there could be no mixture of falsehood.[14] Thus he charged: "For if you mix what is false with what is true, falsehood often imitates the truth by treading in its steps. Just in the same way a picture imitates the true man of nature, depicting with its colors the false resemblance of truth."[15] In other words, since the Catholic bishops are fallen and hence "false," they are unqualified to administer baptism.

To counter this, Augustine accused Petilian of teaching that the baptismal sacrament was made valid by the minister and not by Christ:

> We are neither made fouler by our washing, nor cleaner by yours. But when the water of baptism is given to any one in the name of the Father and of the Son and of the Holy Spirit, it is neither ours nor yours, but His of whom it was said to John, "Upon whom you shall see the Spirit descending, and remaining on Him, the same is He who baptizes with the Holy Ghost."[16]

Augustine makes a valid point, but it does not quite respond to the point the Donatists were making. They were not denying that Christ made the

---

12. Augustine, *Petil.* 2.4: "Bis baptisma nobis obiciunt hi qui sub nomine baptismi animas suas reo lavacro polluerunt, quibus equidem obscenis sordes cunctae mundiores sunt, quos perversa munditia aqua sua contigit inquinari.'"

13. *Petil.* 2.25.58: "Nam cum reus falsa committas, bis baptisma ego non facio quod semel ipse non facis."

14. Burns, *Cyprian,* 10.

15. *Petil.* 2.26.60: "Nam si veris falsa permisceas, isdem saepe vestigiis verum falsitas imitatur. Sic hominem simulat naturae pictura verumque coloribus exprimit falsa facies veritatis."

16. *Petil.* 2.5: "Nec aqua nostra inquinamur nec vestra mundamur, sed aqua baptismi, in nomine Patris et Filii et Spiritus Sancti cum datur alicui, nec nostra nec vestra est, sed illius de quo Iohanni dictum est: 'Super quem videris Spiritum sicut columbam descendentem et manentem super eum, hic est qui baptizat in Spiritu Sancto.'"

baptismal sacrament valid, but rather arguing that an unworthy minister outside the church could not perform a valid sacrament in the first place.

Petilian was also well aware of the advances in Donatist theology made by Parmenian, in particular his teaching concerning the *dotes* that existed in the true Church to validate a sacrament performed by a minister whose sinfulness was unknown to the Church. In his opening, Petilian insisted that we must consider the *conscientia* (the word can mean either "conscience" or "consciousness") of the person receiving the sacrament.[17] If one receives a baptism from a person one knows to be a sinner, then one receives guilt and not faith. If we connect this with Parmenian's Donatist theology, Petilian's statement makes perfect sense. Parmenian argued that if a bishop in the Donatist Church was not holy, the *dotes supplet* would make the sacrament valid nonetheless, on the condition that the church did not know the cleric was a sinner.[18] Petilian builds upon Parmenian's teaching by insisting that it is crucial for individuals being baptized to know what they are receiving. Petilian, like Augustine in *De baptismo,* was trying to discourage his readers from receiving anything from the rival church; he aims to get his listeners to ask why anyone would even think of receiving a sacrament from persons outside the true church. Such persons, however attractive on the surface, have no real faith, do not possess the Holy Spirit, and cannot possibly impart what they do not possess themselves: "Everything (*omnis res*) consists of an origin or root, and, if it have not something for a head, it is nothing and cannot reproduce anything good if it is not itself reproduced from good seed."[19] Petilian thus connects his teaching with the words of Jesus: "'Every good tree brings forth good fruit, but a corrupt tree brings forth evil fruit: do men gather grapes of thorns?' And again, 'A good man, out of the good treasure of his heart, brings forth good things: and an evil man out of the evil treasure, brings forth evil things.'"[20]

17. Monceaux, *Histoire*, 5:311. *Petil.* 1.2: "Nam qui fidem sciens a perfido sumpserit non fidem percipit, sed reatum." Monceaux in an attempt to be true to what Petilian said has added the word *sciens*.

18. See chapter seven for Parmenian's teaching on the church.

19. *Petil.* 2.5.10: "Omnis res enim origine et radice consistit et, si caput non habet aliquid, nihil est, nec quicquam bene regenerat, nisi bono semine regeneretur."

20. *Petil.* 2.5.12: "Dicente domino Iesu Christo: 'Arbor bona fructus bonos facit, arbor mala malos fructus facit. Numquid colligunt de spinis uvas?' et iterum: 'Omnis homo bonus de thesauro cordis sui profert bona, et omnis homo malus de thesauro cordis sui profert mala.'"

Petilian easily connects this with the sacrament of baptism. Just as a corrupt tree cannot bring forth good fruit, in like manner, "he who is baptized by one that is dead, his washing profits him nothing."[21] Moreover, Petilian valued the parable of the good and bad fruit because it rested on the concept of *origo*: Every plant has a seed from which it is sprung; if the seed is bad, it is only because it sprang from a bad source (*origo*). And if the *origo* is bad, the head (*caput*) is useless.[22]

THE CONCEPTS OF *ORIGO* AND *CONSCIENTIA*

The concept of *origo* had existed for some time in African theology. Petilian, like Tertullian and Cyprian before him, used it to buttress his arguments against the opponents of his day. Just as Cyprian could not accept Novatian's group entering the Church without baptism or re-baptism, so Petilian could not accept the Catholics of his day as valid Christians. For such groups had, in the eyes of these African theologians, tried to introduce a source other than the one God gave to the church. For Tertullian it was the Gnostics, for Cyprian the Novatianists, and for Petilian the Catholics—that is, the non-Donatists—who had separated themselves from the true source and as a result had no head (*caput*), no connection with the *origo* of the true church.

Petilian advanced Donatist theology by emphasizing the conscience of the believer and what the individual "knows" while receiving baptism. The idea of one's conscience goes to the concept of *origo*, in that it is related to the administering bishop's holiness or lack thereof. Thus, Petilian sought to use this teaching in his refutation of Augustine. Specifically, in his response to Augustine's letter against him, he insisted that Augustine had omitted a phrase pointing out the fact that he had a bad conscience. Petilian insisted that "if the conscience of him who gives in holiness is what we look for to cleanse the conscience of the recipient then he who has received his faith wittingly from one that is faithless, receives not faith but guilt."[23] It would follow, in Petilian's logic, that because Augustine did not have a good conscience and was not from the right source (*origo*) his head (*caput*) is nothing. Moreover, in Petilian's letter to Augustine

21. *Petil.* 2.7.14: "Et iterum: qui baptizatur a mortuo, non ei prodest lavatio eius."

22. *Petil.* 1.4.5.

23. *Petil.* 3.20.33: "Si conscientia sancte dantis attenditur quae abluat accipientis et qui fidem sciens a perfido sumpserit non fidem percipit sed reatum."

(*Epistula I ad Augustinum*), he accused Augustine of omitting two more words in an attempt to distort the true meaning of his teaching. The words were *sanctes* (holiness) and *sciens* (knowing/ly). Petilian maintained that Augustine intentionally omitted these two words because of his own bad conscience about his baptism. After having read Augustine's *Confessiones*, Petilian argued that Augustine's bad conscience could be attributed to the fact that he had always been a Manichean in secret.[24]

The Donatists repeatedly used against Augustine his admission in his *Confessiones* of having been a Manichean. To Petilian and to other Donatists, Augustine's background had made him no more than a skillful academic who twisted his words to distort the true meaning of his teaching; he was as cunning as a snake, the new Carneades.[25] Although Augustine denied that he had a bad conscience or that he was still a Manichean, the accusation must have had considerable credibility, for some of Augustine's friends were, like Augustine himself, former Manicheans who had become Catholics, as Frend observes: "In 393, Canon 36 of the Council of Hippo was directed against the reading of non-canonical scriptures in church, such as those used by the Manichees. In 400, apart from Augustine himself, his friends, such as the great landowner Romanianus, Alypius bishop of Thagaste, Evodius bishop of Uzaliz, and the successive bishops of Constantine, the capital of Numidia, Profuturus and Fortunatus, were former Manicheans."[26] The last two, in particular, were friends and former students of Augustine at his monastery in Hippo, and Petilian had earlier accused Fortunatus of still being a Manichean—a charge whose believability Augustine himself revealed in one of his letters, admitting that a Catholic sub-deacon had been a Manichean "hearer" for years while ministering to his Catholic congregation without arousing the least suspicion.[27]

More compromising than these suspicions, however, was the letter of Bishop Megalius of Calama challenging Augustine's ordination in 395/6. When Bishop Valerius of Hippo decided to make Augustine his co-adjutor, Megalius objected, doubting the sincerity of Augustine's conversion.[28] Petilian and other Donatists obtained this letter, circulated

24. Courcelle, *Recherches*, 240–42.
25. See chapter 7, n. 46.
26. Frend, "Gnostic-Manichean," 22.
27. Ibid., 23.
28. Frend, "Manichaeism," 864.

copies of it, and insisted that even Catholics suspected the genuineness of Augustine's conversion from Manicheism. In light of this evidence and of the fact that Manicheism was hated in North Africa among both Catholic and Donatist Christians, Petilian's charge must have unsettled Augustine.[29] Moreover, in his response to Augustine (*Epistula I ad Augustinum*), Petilian insisted that Catholics—perhaps from Augustine's own diocese—included a woman who maintained her membership in the Catholic Church while being a catechumen of the Manicheans.[30] Petilian went so far as to accuse Augustine of being not just a secret Manichean but in fact a Manichean presbyter.[31] From Petilian's perspective, these were the reasons why Augustine intentionally omitted the words *sanctes* and *sciens* and the phrase about conscience from his work:[32] Augustine's conversion to the church was not genuine, and he therefore had a bad conscience about his baptism.[33]

Augustine answered Petilian's attacks with some convincing arguments of his own. For example, he offers a biting response, seasoned with a bit of humor, to Petilian's talk of the "root" and "head" of a minister:

> For Petilian expressly states in his epistle, that "everything consists of an origin and root; and if it have not something for a head, it is nothing." And since by the origin and root and head of the baptized person he wishes to be understood the man by whom he is baptized, what good does the unhappy recipient derive from the fact that he does not know how bad a man his baptizer really is? For he does not know that he himself has a bad head, or actually

29. In his *Confessiones*, Augustine tells us how his own mother did not want to let him live with her when she found out he was a Manichean. But God gave Monica a dream that Augustine would eventually be saved, so she relented (3.2.19). Manicheism was disliked by both Donatist and Catholic Christians in North Africa. The Romans also hated Manicheism because it came form Persia, a country against which they had fought some bitter battles.

30. Augustine, *Petil.* 3.17–20.

31. Augustine, *Petil.* 3.17–20: "Me etiam presbyterum fuisse Manicheorum vel falsus vel fallens mirabilis temeritate."

32. Monceaux, *Histoire*, 4:604. In his defense Augustine states: "Let him triumph in my stealing his words, beause I have suppressed two of them, as though the victory were his upon their restoration."

33. Augustine stated in his *Confessiones* (9.8) how angry he was at the Manicheans for having being deceived by their religion—so for Petilian to charge that he was still a Manichean in secret and therefore had a bad conscience about his baptism probably hit a sore spot with Augustine.

no head at all. And yet what hope can a man have, who, whether he is aware of it or not, has either a very bad head or no head at all? Can we maintain that his very ignorance forms a head, when his baptizer is either a bad head or none at all? Surely any one who thinks this is unmistakably without a head.[34]

In challenging Petilian's argument of the bad fruit, Augustine turns Petilian's argument against him: "For if it is as you say, that is, if the fruit of those who baptize consist in baptized persons themselves, you declare a great woe against Africa, if a young Optatus has sprung up from every one that Optatus baptized."[35] Here, Augustine is referring to Bishop Optatus, who, at least from the point of view of the imperial power, was an evil character. So Augustine's accusation is clear: if evil men bear evil fruit, what kind of fruit did this evil man bear among your group? Unfortunately, Augustine found the language of Petilian's critique, *Epistula I ad Augustinum,* so abusive that he did not reproduce it word for word;[36] it would have been interesting to read Petilian's response on this issue. As Frend notes, during the reign of Bishop Optatus, Donatists had reached their zenith in power and prestige, and Optatus himself was well loved and respected by them. When the Maximianists' schism reached its climax and riots broke out among the Donatists, Bishop Optatus intervened and brought an end to the dispute. He demanded that the Primianists and the Maximianists compromise; they did, and the schism ended.[37] Bishop Optatus returned to his diocese of Thamugadi and the Donatist Church celebrated the tenth anniversary of his consecration at its general council. The respect and honor he received at the council speaks to the Donatists' admiration and respect for him. Frend describes the scene as follows:

34. *Petil.* 1.5.6: "'Omnis res enim origine et radice consistit, et si caput non habet aliquid, nihil est,' cumque originem et radicem et caput baptizati hominem a quo baptizatur velit intellegi, quid prodest misero baptizato, quod ignorat quam malus sit baptizator eius? Ignorat enim se malum habere caput aut omnino se esse sine capite. Tamen quae spes est illi, cui sive scienti sive nescienti caput pessimum aut nullum est? Numquid ipsa ignorantia fit ei caput, cui suus baptizator vel malum caput vel nullum est? At hoc quisquis putaverit, vere sine capite est."

35. *Petil.* 2.13: "Nam si ita est, ut dicis, id est fructus baptizantium ipsi baptizati existimantur, magnum malum Africae denuntiatis, si tot Optati pullulaverunt quotquot baptizavit Optatus."

36. *Petil.* 3.1.

37. Frend, *Donatist,* 226. Optatus was a hero to the Donatists and regarded as a martyr by the common people. This Optatus is not to be confused with Optatus of Melevis, a Catholic bishop and author of the anti-Donatist work *De schismate Donatistarum.*

The event struck the imagination of contemporaries. Optatus sat enthroned in state in the raised apse of the vast cathedral which he had probably built, surrounded by his clergy, settling disputes, and, amid the enthusiastic cries of the multitude, letting his will be known to his colleagues by what Augustine describes as *nutu regali*. This moment may well be regarded as the culminating point in the history of the Donatist Church.[38]

Donatists regarded Bishop Optatus as a hero. His ability to lead them through the Maximianists' schism and to challenge rich landowners probably made him a hero among the rest of the native population as well, and not the evil person Augustine suggested he was. Consequently, when Bishop Optatus was executed, the poor people, of whom many were Donatists, honored him as a martyr. Augustine insists repeatedly that Bishop Optatus was a thief and that consequently Petilian was also a thief.[39] Augustine fails to realize, however, that the native population probably saw Optatus' exactions from rich landowners, which Augustine saw as thievery, rather as justice or pay back for years of imperial abuse. Augustine, who was a friend of the local civil officials and somewhat indifferent to the abuses suffered by his own people, could not understand this.[40] His letters, for example, speak of the abuses of the rich landowners against the poor, but he does not seem to appreciate that at some point the latter might be led to rebel. Petilian, being well aware of Augustine's insensitivity on this point, suggested that the bishop of Hippo's African heritage and years of experience should allow him no excuse for his position. Augustine records Petilian's criticism as follows:

So that it should be out of my power to say I was unacquainted with [the situation], he quotes Mensurius, Caecilianus, Macarius, Taurinus, Romanus, and declares that they had acted in opposition to the church of God, as I could not fail to know, seeing that I am an African, and already well advanced in years.[41]

38. Frend, *Donatist*, 223.

39. *Petil.* 2.53.

40. In *Ep.* 108.6. and 18 Augustine describes in detail the problems of the Donatists but cannot seem to acknowledge wrong done by the Catholics. As Frend notes, "Augustine was conservative and a defender of established order, including slavery." Frend, *Donatist*, 64.

41. *Petil.* 3.30.29: "Ne mihi liceat dicere: 'Ignoravi,' commemorat Mensurium, Caecilianum, Macarium, Taurinum, Romanum, et eos contra ecclesiam Dei fecisse affirmat quae ignorare non possem, eo quod Afer sim et aetate paene iam senex."

Petilian points out that, as an elderly African, Augustine should know of the abuses of the Roman government against the church in North Africa and that even if Augustine did not agree with the theology of the Donatists, he should at least acknowledge the abuses committed at the hands of Macarius, Taurinus or Romanus. Because Augustine could not understand this, he not only condemned the rebellions of Firmus and Gildo but also failed to criticize the oppressive measures taken by Roman officials, even such vicious officials as those mentioned.[42] Indeed, in response to Petilian, Augustine defended them: "But whatever Macarius and Taurinus and Romanus did, either in their judicial or executive functions, in behalf of unity as against their pertinacious madness, it is beyond doubt that it was all done in accordance with the laws, which these same persons made it unavoidable should be passed and put in force, by referring the case of Caecilianus to the judgment of the emperor."[43]

Here the political, social, economic, and theological assumptions held by each group could not be overcome. Consequently, a religious leader who tried to bring a certain measure of political and social justice could be a hero to one group and a thief to the other. Because Augustine could not understand this, many of his arguments that he felt skillfully refuted his opponents no doubt fell on deaf ears.

THE MAXIMIANIST SCHISM: A SIN AGAINST GOD OR HUMAN BEINGS?

Another argument which Augustine used repeatedly to refute the Donatists' teaching on rebaptism and persecution was their handling

---

Concerning Augustine's lack of knowledge regarding African church history see *Ep.* 44. Here Augustine writes to his friend regarding Fortunius, a bishop with whom Augustine engaged in a rather civil debate, in the course of which Fortunius informed Augustine that the Donatists tried to avoid a schism by having an administrator in Carthage before Majorinus, but that the Catholics murdered him in his church. To this revelation, Augustine said, "I admit that I had never heard of this before, though our side rejects and refutes so many charges raised by them and hurls more and greater charges at them."

42. Firmus rebelled against the abuses of the Roman government, and Gildo rebelled for his dream of having Africa for the Africans. On the other hand, Count Romanus was so abusive in his rule that neither Rome nor the Africans liked him.

43. *Petil.* 3.25.29: "Macarius vero et Taurinus et Romanus quidquid vel iudiciaria vel executoria potestate adversus eorum obstinatum furorem pro unitate fecerunt, secundum leges eos fecisse constat, quas idem ipsi causam Caeciliani ad imperatoris iudicium deferendo contra se ferri exerique coegerunt."

of the Maximianist schism. In his answer to Petilian, he mentions this schism no less than fifteen times in book two alone.[44] In fact, when it appears that he does not have an adequate answer to a particular argument, he refers back to the Maximianist schism. But once again we must ask whether Augustine fully understood the Donatists' position on this issue.

During the last decade of the fourth century, a Donatist deacon named Maximian brought charges against his bishop, Primian, for inappropriate conduct. When this was brought to the attention of other bishops, Bishop Primian succeeded in getting some of his fellow bishops to side with him against Maximian, who in the meantime had gotten himself consecrated a bishop. However, Bishop Felicianus of Musti sided with Maximian at the council of June 24, 393, in which Primian was condemned by a group of one hundred bishops. In the major Donatist areas, such as Numidia and Mauretania, Primian nonetheless had considerable support. As a result, a universal council of the Donatist Church was summoned on April 25, 394. It reversed Primian's condemnation and in the most solemn terms excommunicated Maximian and twelve of his coadjutors who had consecrated him bishop, together with the Carthaginian clergy who supported him; but it offered reconciliation to those excommunicated if they made their peace with the church by Christmas of that year. Maximian and the other dissidents availed themselves of this opportunity and "were allowed to return as bishops to the main Donatist body, bringing with them, without requirements of rebaptism, all whom they had baptized."[45] Augustine comments on the apparent contradiction between this action and the Donatist teaching on baptism, singling out Bishop Felicianus of Musti who had sided with Maximian:

> In the next place, in that council of yours in which you condemned Maximianus with his advisers or his ministers, have you forgotten with what eloquence you said, "Even after the manner of the Egyptians, the shores are full of the bodies of the dying, on whom the weightier punishments fall than death itself, in that, after their life has been wrung from them by the avenging waters, they have not found so much as burial," And yet you yourselves

44. In 2.15 (once), 2.35 (three times), 2.43 (once), 2.45 (three times), 2.48 (once), 2.106 (once), 2.132 (three times), 2.134 (once), 2.184 (once). In nearly all of his writings against the Donatists Augustine mentioned the Maximianist schism. Moreover, at the conference in Carthage in 411, Augustine used the Maximianist schism as one of his main arguments against the Donatists.

45. Frend, *Donatist*, 218.

may see whether or not one of them, Felicianus, has been brought to life again; yet he had with him within the communion of your body those whom he baptized outside. As therefore he is baptized by One that is alive, who is clothed with the baptism of the living Christ, so he is baptized by the dead who is wrapped in the baptism of the dead Saturn, or any one like him; that we may set forth in the meanwhile, with what brevity we may, in what sense the words which you have quoted may be understood without any caviling on the part of any one of us. For, in the sense in which they are received by you, you make no effort to explain them, but only strive to entangle us together with yourselves.[46]

In Augustine's *Retractiones* (which means "re-treatments," not "retractions" in the current English sense), he admits that in 397 he was not a real specialist (*nondum expertus*) in the Donatist theory of baptism.[47] However, when Augustine entered the debate against the Donatists, he began studying Donatist literature and challenging Donatist bishops to a debate. He also sought to use any schism or quarrel within their ranks to expose any weakness in their teaching. As noted earlier, when Parmenian excommunicated Tyconius, Augustine sided with Tyconius against his former bishop, Parmenian. And when Augustine learned of the Maximianist schism, he believed he had found the perfect argument to refute his opponents. Consequently, he went to great lengths to secure accurate information about this incident. As Frend points out, Augustine "visited the main centers of Maximianism in the Mejerda valley to obtain first-hand accounts of events, in order to argue more effectively Donatist inconsistencies in their treatment of Maximianists and Catholics."[48] For the next several years Augustine would use this schism repeatedly to refute the Donatist teaching on rebaptism. It is true that the Donatists seemed

---

46. *Petil.* 2.16: "Deinde in illo concilio vestro, quo Maximianum cum suis auctoribus vel suis ministris damnastis, excidit tibi quam eloquenter dixeritis: 'Aegyptiorum admodum exemplo pereuntium funeribus plena sunt litora, quibus in ipsa morte maior est poena, quod post extortam aquis ultricibus animam nec ipsam inveniunt sepulturam.' Et tamen unus eorum Felicianus utrum revixerit vos videritis, secum tamen apud vos intus habet quos foris mortuus baptizavit. Sicut ergo a vivo baptizatur qui vivi Christi baptismo induitur, sic a mortuo baptizatur qui mortui Saturni vel cuiuslibet alterius baptismo involvitur, ut interim cito dicamus, quomodo verba quae posuisti sine cuiusquam nostrum angustia possint intellegi. Nam sicut accipiuntur a vobis, non vos explicare, sed nos vobiscum implicare contenditis."

47. *Retr.* 1.21.

48. Frend, *Donatist*, 237.

to be inconsistent in the way they dealt with the Maximianist schismatics on one hand and with their Catholic rivals on the other. However, the Maximianist schism was an issue of schismatic bishops within their own ranks, rather than that of lapsed or traitor clergy who were considered outside the church and, in Donatist eyes, stained with a contagious sin or, as Petilian said, with a bad *conscientia*. Moreover, Augustine missed the important distinction that for the Donatists the schismatic members of their own church had sinned against human beings, whereas Caecilian and the Catholics had sinned against God. Consequently, as Schindler suggests, the differing treatment of Maximianists and Catholics did not reflect a true contradiction in Donatist theology.[49]

WHERE IS THE AFRICAN CHURCH: WITH THE PERSECUTORS OR WITH THE PERSECUTED?

Another major theme in Petilian's polemic is the use of violence. He severely criticized Catholic Christians of North Africa for their desire to persecute the Donatist Church. In Petilian's view, this behavior revealed how corrupt Catholics had become. He charged that "there is no fellowship of darkness with light, nor any fellowship of bitterness with the sweet of honey;" hence, there should be no fellowship with the Catholics for

> they went out from us, but they were not of us; for if they had been of us, they would no doubt have continued with us (I John 2:19) . . . For it is written, As gold is tried in the furnace, so also are the just by the harassing of tribulation. Cruelty is not a part of gentleness, nor religion a part of sacrilege; nor can the party of Macarius in any way be part of us, because he pollutes the likeness of our rite.[50]

The true Christians should not only expect persecution but also understand that they are made pure by harassing and tribulation, as gold is made pure by the heat of fire. Similarly, the party of the persecutors, that

---

49. Schindler, "L'histoire," 1313: "Maximianus avait péché contre un homme, Caecilianus contre Dieu."

50. *Petil.* 2.39.92: "Ex nobis prodierunt, sed non erant ex nobis, nam, si fuissent ex nobis, permansissent utique nobiscum. Scriptum est namque: 'Sicut aurum probat fornax, ita et iustos vexatio tribulationis.' Non est pars crudelitas mansuetudinis nec religio sacrilegii nec pars Macari penitus potest esse nostra, quia ritus nostri similitudinem maculat."

is, the party of Macarius and the Catholics, can in no way be a part of the true church.

Petilian used the scriptures to criticize his opponents' use of force, but none so forcefully as the Beatitudes:

> But wherein do you fulfill the commandments of God? The Lord Christ said, "Blessed are the poor in spirit; for theirs is the kingdom of heaven." But you by your malice in persecution breathe forth the riches of madness. . . ."Blessed are the meek, for they shall inherit the earth." You therefore, not being meek, have lost both heaven and earth alike. . . . "Blessed are they that mourn: for they shall be comforted." You, our butchers, are the cause of mourning in others; you do not mourn yourselves . . . "Blessed are they which do hunger and thirst after righteousness; for they shall be filled." To you it seems to be righteousness that you thirst after our blood.[51]

Petilian continues throughout his pastoral letter to demonstrate by scripture and previous historical accounts that the persecuting Catholics should be avoided at all costs, for they are not followers of scripture, nor are they followers of Christ, because they do not follow his example:

> But I answer you, on the other hand, that Jesus Christ never persecuted any one, and when the apostles found fault with certain parties, and suggested that He should have recourse to persecution (He Himself having come to create faith by inviting men to Him, rather than by compelling them), the apostles say, "Many lay on hands in Thy name, and are not with us"; but Jesus says, "Let them alone: if they are not against you, they are on your side."[52]

Petilian persuasively dispels all justification for persecution by his opponents. Not only are Catholics not following Jesus' example, but

51. *Petil.* 2.63.141: "Divina vero manadata quibus rebus impletis? Dicit Dominus Christus: 'Beati pauperes spiritu, quoniam ipsorum est regnum caelorum.' Vos persequendi malitia furoris divitias exhalatis." 2.64.143: "'Beati mansueti, quoniam ipsi possidebunt terram.' Vos igitur non mansueti terram et caelum pariter perdidistis." 2.65.145: "'Beati qui lugent, quoniam ipsi consolabuntur.' Vos, nostri carnifices, lugentes facitis, non lugetis." 2.66.147: "'Beati qui esuriunt et sitiunt iustitiam, quoniam ipsi saturabuntur.' Vobis haec iustitia est, ut nostrum sanguinem sitiatis."

52. *Petil.* 2. 177: "Ego vero e contra respondeo Iesum Christum neminem persecutum, et cum aliquae sectae apostolis eidem suggerentibus displicerent—ita enim fidem venerat facere, ut non cogeret homines, sed potius invitaret—dicunt illi apostoli: 'Multi in nomine tuo manus imponunt et nobiscum non sunt.' Dixit Iesus: 'Dimittite illos; si contra vos non sunt, pro vobis sunt.'"

they are hypocritical in their practices. Finally, like a lawyer setting up his witness, Petilian gives Augustine and other Catholics an alternative: "Choose, in short, which of the two alternatives you prefer. If innocence is on your side, why do you persecute us with the sword? Or if you call us guilty why do you, who are yourselves innocent, seek for our company?"[53]

In his reply to Petilian, Augustine refused to choose between these alternatives; instead, he chose both. Understanding that Petilian had skillfully backed Catholics into a corner, he pleaded innocent, not only evading an answer to Petilian's question but also insisting that Catholics were innocent of persecuting Donatists, while the Donatists were guilty of persecuting Catholics. Each time Petilian attacked Catholics for persecuting Donatists, Augustine would remind Petilian of Bishop Optatus, the Circumcellions, or the Maximianist schism, as if this refuted Petilian's claim that the Catholics were persecutors. Many of Augustine's answers were thus evasive and redundant.

Why could not Augustine at some point admit Catholics had persecuted the Donatists? I suggest that Augustine could not admit this because he himself had previously requested aid from the imperial authorities and at the time of this correspondence (400–403) was planning other ways he could influence imperial powers against the Donatists. Consequently, since Augustine and the Catholics had used secular power to persecute the Donatists, the best argument Augustine could make is that the Donatists' party was also guilty of persecution.

On the other hand, Petilian would not admit that the Circumcellions or other persons within his party were guilty of persecuting the Catholics. It is therefore understandable why much of what both parties wrote or said carried little weight with the other. Augustine's call for unity must have rung hallow with Petilian, because Petilian could too easily accuse the bishop of Hippo of hypocrisy and worse, as indeed he did:

> For even if you do not murder a man with your hands, you do so with your butcherous tongues. All, men therefore, who have been murdered, you, the instigator of the deed, have slain. Nor indeed does the hand of the butcher glow save at the instigation of your tongue and that terrible heart of the breast is inflamed by

---

53. *Petil.* 2.97.220: "Eligite tandem de duobus alterum quid dicatis. Si innocentia vobis est, cur nos ferro sectamini? aut si reos nos, quid nos quaeritis innocentes?"

your words to take the blood of others—blood that shall take a just vengeance upon him who shed it."[54]

Petilian's words proved prophetic. For in 404, the Catholic Church held a council that asked the emperor to declare Donatism no longer a schism but a heresy. The emperor agreed and in 405, promulgated the Edict of Unity, which among other things declared the practice of rebaptism unlawful and in effect outlawed the Donatist Church.[55]

One may be tempted to conclude with Frend "that by all tests, the Catholics were the schismatics and traitors to the church."[56] They certainly encouraged imperial force to destroy those that did not join their ranks and declared that force was justified when a few Donatists yielded to it and became Catholics.[57]

The exchange of the two leaders, however, makes clear that each man sincerely believed that his group represented the true Catholic Church. Moreover, Augustine was every bit as obsessed with having Donatists return to the Catholic Church as Donatists were obsessed with rebaptizing Catholics who joined their congregations. Both men were impressive writers and could twist an argument to fit the occasion. Yet neither of them would accept or even acknowledge any weakness in his own position or the merits of his opponents' factual points—such as the persecution of Catholics by Circumcellions on behalf of the Donatists or the encouragement by Catholics of imperial persecution of Donatists. For this reason, meaningful dialogue was impossible. Furthermore, Augustine did not fully appreciate the distinctions in his opponent's theology. In almost every case, he missed the point Petilian was making. It is therefore no surprise that Donatists were not impressed with what Augustine had to say. And it is no surprise that if Augustine wanted to win, he had to use the imperial authorities to do so. Consequently, what Augustine could

54. *Petil.* 2.202: "Non desinitis iugulare, non enim, si tamen manu non facitis, lingua carnifice hominem iugulatis. Scriptum est enim: 'Mors et vita in manibus linguae.' Omnes ergo qui occisi sunt tu qui suasor es occidisti. Neque enim manus carnificis nisi lingua tua fervescit et ille durus pectoris calor in alienum sanguinem verbis tuis accenditur, sanguinem iustum sui vindicem diffusorum."

55. Willis, *Augustine*, 130.

56. Frend, *Donatist*, 255.

57. Augustine, *Ep.* 185.2.11. This letter is one of many examples of Augustine's justification for persecution of the Donatists. Augustine belives his cause is one of "righteous persecution, which the Church of Christ inflicts upon the impious."

not accomplish through debate or the pen, he influenced the strong arm of the law to implement by force. And like his counterpart, Augustine invoked chosen scriptures to justify his position.[58] On this point, the criticism made by Petilian and other Donatists that Augustine was the new Carneades was probably correct.

---

58. On Augustine's justification of coercion, see Willis, *Augustine*, 127–43.

9

Imperial Repression, African Resilience:
Where is the Church?

THE EDICT OF UNITY, 405 CE

FROM THE 390S AND into the first decades of the 400s, Augustine and other Catholics made strenuous efforts to have the Donatists subject to existing heresy laws. The Catholics were not successful initially, but with persistence they were able to win and sustain two major victories against the Donatists in 405 and 411. During this time they had the backing of the government, so they began to exert various forms of pressure on their opponents. First, the Catholics tried to force the Donatists into a debate in which civil authorities favorable to their side would be the judges. Second, Catholics went into Donatist territories preaching and winning converts. Finally, some Catholic bishops engaged in legal proceedings to confiscate Donatist churches. In response, the Donatists increased their acts of violence. This played into the hands of the Catholics, for it allowed them to present themselves as victims before the authorities, when they were in fact often the real instigators.

At some point before 403, the Donatist bishop Restitutus agreed to change his allegiance and join the Catholic Church. As a result, he was beaten, humiliated, and held captive by Donatist militants.[1] Proculeianus, the Donatist bishop of Hippo, arranged after two weeks for Restitutus's release, having been informed that the Catholics were going to press charges unless he resolved the matter. Restitutus was released, but Augustine still issued a formal protest, and Proculeianus was summoned before the au-

---

1. Augustine, *Ep.* 88.8. Around the same time, Augustine was also the target of an attack by Donatist militants, but he took the wrong road and escaped injury. Hermanowicz, *Possidius,*137.

thorities. Proculeianus asked that the investigation be waived, and he was sent home.[2] Augustine tried repeatedly to summon Proculeianus back before the local authorities but without success. Augustine planned to argue that Proculeianus, rather then the kidnappers, was legally responsible because the incident happened in his jurisdiction. Erica Hermanowicz believes this is one of Augustine's earliest attempts to use the heresy laws against a Donatist bishop. Augustine was not successful in this case, but he would soon have another chance.[3]

A Catholic council in 403 agreed to try to force the Donatists into a debate before the authorities. When several Donatist bishops were approached about this invitation, the Donatists too held a council, at which they agreed to refuse to meet with their Catholic rivals, believing that "it was unworthy that the sons of the martyrs and the children of the traitors come together."[4] At that time, the Donatists were the majority church in North Africa and were content with being left to themselves, but this proved impossible. In a new move, the Catholics had their bishop Possidius publicly criticize the hot-tempered Donatist bishop Crispinus for refusing to debate with him. Since because of the decision of the Donatist council Crispinus could not engage in a debate with Possidius, the Donatist chose another means to exact revenge for his humiliation: he had some of his comrades attack Possidius a few days later. Possidius was severely beaten, but his life was spared. When the news of the attack circulated among the people, Crispinus had to report the incident to the authorities but said he would handle the situation through the church. When he did not follow though with this pledge, Possidius decided (probably at Augustine's urging) to bring charges of heresy against Crispinus. When Crispinus was initially tried for heresy, he denied that he was a heretic, and the proconsul agreed. However, when this proconsul was replaced, the Catholics came up with another plan. Augustine requested that the new proconsul listen to the two bishops debate. Either Possidius was very convincing in the debate or the outcome had been fixed, for Crispinus was declared a heretic and fined ten pounds of gold according to the law of 392 regarding heretics.[5] After this victory, Possidius asked that the fine against Crispinus

2. Augustine, *Ep.* 88.8, 105.3.

3. Hermanowicz, *Possidius*, 180.

4. Ibid., 111.

5. Ibid., 116.

be waived, since it was not money but the right to use heresy laws against Donatist bishops that the Catholics wanted. This put Crispinus and the Donatists in a serious dilemma. They objected to the decision, but should they appeal it to the emperor? Hermanowicz explains the dilemma they faced:

> Crispinus and the Donatists had no choice but to appeal. Aside from theological considerations and the understandable rejection of the appellation "heretic," acceptance of the ruling gave the Catholics the precedent they needed to pursue all Donatist bishops and landowners with heavy monetary fines. The importance of this case is underscored by the fact that the decision to appeal was not made at Crispinus' basilica at Calama, but was an expression of collective opinion among the Donatist hierarchy.[6]

When Crispinus did appeal his case to the emperor, Emperor Honorius declared that Crispinus and the Donatists were accountable to the laws against heretics. Bishop Crispinus was ordered to pay the fine of ten pounds of gold, as were the proconsul and staff who had not enforced the law before Crispinius' appeal. The Catholics succeeded in getting the penalty against the proconsul and his staff waived. The ground was now laid for anti-Donatist legislation. According to Augustine, when the emperor saw the terrible wounds inflected on Catholic bishops by Donatist militants, he decided to enforce the heresy legislation himself.[7] Augustine tried to distance himself from the enactment of this law, as he had done repeatedly against previous accusations by Petilian. Hermonowicz, however, challenges this assertion by Augustine: "Not only do the laws, including the Edict of Unity, seems to emerge from the consistory only after the delegation arrived, but the Latin indicates the arrival of the bishops was coterminous with the bishop of Bagai's dramatic appearance."[8] With this legal victory against them, the Donatists faced another great challenge. Hermanowicz summarizes the situation:

---

6. Ibid., 116.

7. Augustine, *Ep.* 88.7: "But when the legation came to Rome, the horrible and quite recent scars of the Catholic bishop of Bagai moved the emperor to issue the sort of laws that we now have."

8. Hermanowicz, *Possidius*, 150: "Honorius published the Edict of Unity and the other anti-Donatist directives in February 405 (preserved, in part, in the *Theodosian Code* as 16.5.38, 16.6.3 [the Edict proper], 16.6.4, 16.6.5 and 16.11.2)."

The Edict of Unity is a harsh document containing much more uncompromising language than the other letters issued in February
and March of 405. This directive alone (as far as we can tell from
what survives of the texts) lumped the Donatists together with the
Manicheans and states that those persevering in the practice of
heretical worship were subject to laws previously enacted against
them, specifically those issued by Honorius. Donatists were now
subject to all antiheretical legislation, including those against the
Manichaeans, which since the days of Diocletian had been particularly stringent. The Edict also states that if seditious mobs
assembled, "sharp goads of a more severe punishment will be
applied."[9]

The 405 Edict of Unity severely hindered the Donatists' ability to
function as a church, and for the next three years (405–408) many of their
bishops had to go unto hiding as they secretly directed their churches.
However, political instability would soon turn things in the Donatists'
favor. In 408, several civil officials at home and abroad were executed.
When this happened, the Donatists reasserted themselves with a vengeance.[10] Augustine wrote around this time that the situation in Africa
had—from the Catholics' viewpoint—deteriorated.[11] To get things back
in order, he requested from Olympius (Stilichos' replacement, and a
staunch supporter of the Catholics) that he reaffirm the anti-heresy laws
enacted in 405 against the Donatists. Augustine was not disappointed,
for in November 408 and January 409, Emperor Honorius reinstated the
laws of 405 and added the death penalty for anyone who violated them.
In addition, the new proconsul of Africa, Donatus, intended to carry out
the letter of the law and enforce the death penalty when appropriate. At
this point, however, Augustine demurred, politely informing Donatus
that the Catholics did not want the death penalty enforced against their
rivals. Donatus simply ignored Augustine and did not reply to his letter.

9. Hermanowicz, *Possidius,* 151.

10. Frend, *Donatist,* 270. Concerning the change of events, Frend has this to say:
"In Northern Numidia and Proconsular Africa there was a general outburst against the
Catholic delegages to the Imperial Court in 404. Two bishops, Macarius and Severus,
were killed, and apparently in the same incident the Catholic delegates to the Imperial
Court in 404, Evodius and Theasius, were severely beaten. Other clergy had to flee for
their lives and were forced to seek refuge at Ravenna. Converts from Donatism were
subjected to murderous assaults. Gildo's former sympathizers began to stir again, and
Gildo's memory was once more celebrated."

11. Augustine, *Ep.* 97.

By making this request, Augustine was asking Donatus to ignore the very laws which both Augustine and his fellow bishops had solicited. This is, however, not as inconsistent as it might seem, for Augustine wanted to have it both ways: he wanted to have the Donatists punished as heretics but not persecuted in any way that would allow them to become martyrs or claim that they were suffering for righteousness.[12]

To add to the confusion, Olympius himself was executed in 409 while Alaric had threatened Rome twice. Honorius, being grateful for the African provinces' loyalty, forgave them their back taxes and allowed a certain degree of religious toleration, which the Donatists exploited to their advantage.[13] The new Donatist bishop in Hippo, Macrobius, "openly processed into the city and reoccupied a church that, until recently, had been under Catholic control."[14] This action prompted the Catholics to send a delegation to Ravenna in 410 requesting that the emperor clarify his laws against the Donatists and order a general council between the two parties with an imperial representative as overseer. This request was granted.

THE CONFERENCE OF CARTHAGE, 411 CE

On February 1, 3 and 8 of June 411 the African churches came to-gether under the direction of Flavius Marcellinus, the agent of Emperor Honorius. The Donatists quickly realized that they were neither in a regu-lar church council where every bishop could speak and participate nor in a strictly legal proceeding in which there was a plaintiff and a defendant.[15] To their humiliation, they learned that they were in a conference destined for their condemnation. At the start of the meeting, the emperor's rescript was read that openly condemned the Donatists as liars and their beliefs

12. Hermanowicz, *Possidius*, 187. Augustine's request put the local officials at odds with the laws of the emperor. When the emperor found Crispinus to be a heretic, he fined not only the bishop but also the local officials who had not enforced the law. The Catholics were able to get the fines on the officials overturned, but future officials such as Donatus were aware of this precedent and wanted to avoid putting themselves at odds with the emperor.

13. Frend, *Donatist*, 273.

14. Hermanowicz, *Possidius*, 190–91. See Augustine, *Ep.* 108.14.

15. Tilley, "Dilartory Donatists," 9–10. Tilley notes that the Donatists were under the impression that the meeting would be held as a church council, but enroute to the conference Marcellinus issued a new instruction, allowing delegates from each side to represent their party.

as false (1.5). And the term "Catholic" (the application of which was supposed to be determined at this meeting) had been assigned beforehand to Augustine's group. When the Donatist leaders complained, Marcellinus said he was following the emperor's dictates. Marcellinus was polite to the Donatists, but "the parameters for the case as established by the imperial rescript made it impossible for the Donatists to escape condemnation."[16] What were they to do? Augustine later criticized the Donatists for wasting time and stalling during the proceedings, and many scholars have agreed with his assessment. However, more recent scholars, such as Tilley and Hermanowicz, have seen some merit in the Donatists' approach to the conference.

Having been forced to attend a conference in which they were destined to be condemned, the Donatists tried their best to work within the Roman legal system to have the proceedings dismissed. For example, they correctly noted that their rivals had arrived several days after the appointed start date for the conference: the Catholics had arrived on May 25, while the emperor had ordered the conference to start on May 19. Thus, the Donatists argued that according to the rules of procedure the case should be dismissed.[17] Marcellinus countered by saying that he had ordered the parties to convene on June 1 but that the emperor had given him liberty to extend the deadline two months. The Donatists responded that if they had been the late party their Catholic rivals would have insisted that they forfeit the case. To this, Marcellinus and the Catholics made no reply.[18]

Since the Donatists could not get the case dismissed, they proceeded to the next issue they believed central to their defense. They wanted to settle which party was the defendant and which party was the plaintiff in the case. The Donatists considered themselves the defendants because they had been summoned to the conference as a result of charges brought against them by their Catholic rivals, and they insisted on knowing what Possidius and the Catholic delegation had told the emperor the year before. This was important for at least two reasons: first, if they could prove that their opponents lied to the emperor or misstated facts, then they could request that the case be dismissed; and second, if they knew exactly

16. Hermanowicz, *Possidius*, 196.

17. *Gesta* 1.29, 3.203–7. The edition of the *Gesta* used is Lancel, ed., *Actes*.

18. Hermanowicz, *Possidius*, 206.

what they were being accused of, they could properly defend themselves before the imperial agent. Unfortunately, no matter how much they insisted, Marcellinus would not allow either that the record concerning the Catholic delegation in 410 be read or that the Donatists be designated as defendants at the conference. Thus, the Donatists were not allowed the legal rights of a defendant, but were treated as defendants nonetheless.[19] In protest, during each day of the proceedings the Donatists refused to be seated when asked. In imitation of Christ, who stood before Pilate, they too stood before their accusers.

The Donatists next raised the issue of the manner in which the Catholics wanted the conference to proceed—an issue that turned out to be related to the question of Christian identity around which the whole debate revolved. Marcellinus's edict characterized the *Collatio* as a civil procedure and not a church council, but it was left to the participants to decide how the conference would proceed.[20] Petilian argued that a Christian was not supposed to take another Christian to court and that to do so would indicate that that person was not a Christian. Moreover, in Petilian's view, Christians should use the law of God, not arguments from civil law, to decide their differences: "If [my adversary] separates himself from the law of God, he demonstrates that he is not a bishop, but if he truly desires to hold to the law [of God], I must answer him as a man who desires to be a Christian."[21] Petilian skillfully challenged his Catholic rivals here; for if they admitted that they were plaintiffs arguing against fellow Christians under civil law, then they would confess to disobeying divine law and forfeiting their right to be called Christian or Catholic. In response, however, Augustine demonstrated his acumen also: he agreed not to make the conference a civil proceeding if the Donatists would agree not to bring up evidence about specific persons, such as Caecilian or the various people they believed were *traditores*.[22] As Tilley notes, this presented a new dilemma for the Donatists:

> On the one hand, if they opted for the method of argumentation
> they preferred, Scripture, they would lose some of their best evi-

19. Hermanowicz, *Possidius*, 203.

20. Tilley, "Dilatory Donatists," 13.

21. *Gesta* 2.53: "Si a lege discesserit, episcopum se non esse demonstrat; si vero legem tenuerit, tunc ei ut illi qui christianus esse desiderat respondere." When Petilian mentioned this point again, Augustine reponded in *Gesta* 3.153 (1.53).

22. *Gesta* 3.156.

dence, the very basis of the schism as far as they were concerned, namely, the Caecilianist controversy. On the other hand, if they introduced material from their Caecilianist dossier, they would find themselves engaged in a civil suit and unable to use Scripture as the basis for their case. Neither alternative was satisfying because their ecclesiology was both scriptural and exceptionally personal.[23]

In the end, however, both parties agreed to use scripture.

WHERE IS THE TRUE CHURCH?

Although both parties finally agreed to use scripture, the conference at Carthage is not full of theological argumentation. If that were so, it would be a treasure to historians, for all the leading bishops in Africa were present there. On the other hand, both parties discussed in some detail the topic of this book: "Where is the church?" Augustine insisted that his party represented the true Catholic Church because it was in communion with churches throughout the world and not just with those of Africa.[24] In response, the Donatist bishop Emeritus insisted that the Donatists did not claim that there were no true churches outside of Africa, but only that those churches in communion with the Donatists' rivals in Africa were in communion with the wrong church.[25] Moreover, Emeritus argued that what happened outside of Africa could not prejudice their case, since their disagreement was among Africans.

The Catholics also argued that the parable of the wheat and the tares (Matt 13:24–30) showed that the church consisted of sinners and saints and that God would separate the two groups at the end of the world. The "tares," in their understanding, represented the sinners within the church, thus allowing for a mixed church with both sinners and saints. The Donatists, on the other hand, interpreted the "tares" and the "wheat" to represent respectively the world at large and the church, so that the parable did not justify the presence of sinners in the church. Similarly, the Catholics interpreted the parable of the dragnet of fishes (Matt 13:47–50) to indicate that the good and bad fish remained together until the end of

23. Tilley, "Dilatory Donatists," 13.

24. *Gesta*, 3.100–101.

25. Tilley, "Dilatory Donatists," 17. See *Gesta* 3.99: "cum inter Afros hoc negotium ventiletur."

the voyage—that is, in their understanding, until the end of the world. This interpretation likewise allowed both sinners and saints to exist in the church. The Donatists, however, maintained that as soon as the fish are raised above the waterline and the boat reaches land, their identity is discovered. Tilley clarifies the Donatist position on this point:

> By emphasizing timing, they capitalized on the very words of the gospel: "The Evangelist labels '*hidden*' those you called 'mixed.'" For the Donatists, only when the character of the fish or the sinner became *known* was that identity crucial. The Catholics, in Donatist eyes, were unable to deal with evil when it had been identified. On these grounds the Donatists could claim to be the true church even if their congregations contained sinners, for they dealt with them as soon as they were identified.[26]

Petilian also argued that the Donatists were the true church because of the Catholics' lack of veracity:

> That the Catholic Church is in my possession, both our pure form of worship as well as your sins and your outrages makes true. The whole church of God will be under obligation to be pure, holy, without stain or wrinkle. That is why, therefore, so that we may agree to a discussion of this matter and utilize at the appropriate time divine testimony the first matter of business is—that I ask from you, if you have enough confidence, especially since our most just judge is conducting this part of the case—that whatever must be done be disseminated among the people. It is clear enough that you lied to our most clement emperor, since you hesitate to reveal what you said, what you did, what you ordered, what that legate assumed, what mandate he accepted, what he accomplished. Let the consciousness of the people know these things, let all the provinces know, let the *acta* and this controversy fully preserve it, let them know that you most evidently have no faith in your lie and that you tie delays on to the proceedings so that, by your deception and obstructive trifles it may never arrive at the truth.[27]

26. Ibid., 17. The Donatist teaching on baptism insists that what people know about the person baptizing them matters. In Donatist theology, one is responsible for what one knows. See chapter 8, "Petilian: True Versus False Baptism."

27. *Gesta* 3.75: "Ecclesiam catholicam penes me esse, et pura observatio nostra facit et vitia vestra atque fagitia vestra. Omnis ecclesia Dei pura, sancta, sine macula et ruga esse debebit. Quare igitur, ut ad huius disputationem rei possimus descendere et congruo tempore testimoniis dominicis uti, prius est—quod de te flagito, si non diffidis, maxime cum id agat causae iustissimus cognitor—ut quicquid agendum sit populo publicetur.

Petilian here used an argument he had used against Augustine some ten years earlier. Toward the end of his charge, he insists that all people should be informed of the many lies of the Catholics, thus implying that when people know the truth, they will make the right judgment concerning the church and this conference, even if the civil authorities do not.[28] He thus appealed to the people and to future generations who would read the transcripts of this conference and decide for themselves who represented the true church in North Africa.

When the conference concluded, the Donatists were condemned as planned and it was decreed that their churches were to be handed over to their Catholic rivals unless they agreed to give up their "error." Although the exact numbers of the converts from Donatism to the "official" church are not known, it is clear that there were no mass conversions to the Catholic side. Moreover, the leading Donatist bishops remained steadfast in their defiance, in spite of severe persecution.[29] The Donatists certainly outlived Augustine, and there is evidence that the Donatist Church existed well into the sixth century. For example, in 591 Pope Gregory received reports of Donatist bishops bribing Catholic bishops so they could establish churches in several towns in southern Numidia. And for the next six years Pope Gregory addresses this concern in several letters.[30] After this incident, we have no other record of Donatist activity. We can assume however, that Donatism existed beyond this emergence, but how long and to what extent we are not certain.

Mentitum te igitur clementissimo imperatori sat constat, cum dubitas proferre quid dixeris, quid egeris, quid mandaveris, quid susceperit ille legatus, quid mandatum acceperit, quid peregerit. Noverit haec conscientia populi, sciat universa provincia, hoc acta istaque controversia plene contineant, sciant vos apertissime de mendacio vestro diffidere morasque innectere actioni, ne ad veritatem aliquando vestris praestigiis nebulisque obstantibus veniatur." Translation from Hermanowicz, *Possidius*, 213–14.

28. Hermanowicz, *Possidus*, 214: "There are at least seven occasions during the conference when the Donatists accuse the Catholics of lying."

29. One documented example of the persecution the Donatists faced happened around 429: "Dulcitius arrived at Thamugadi and demanded the surrender of the Donatist cathedral. He was met with a blunt refusal. Supported by his congregation, Gaudentius retired to the safety of the walls of his citadel whence, from its position on a vantage-point overlooking the whole town, he could defy the authorities. In the event of force being used, he declared his intention of burning the building with himself and everyone else inside." The official summoned Augustine, but he was not successful in convincing the Donatist to surrender. Frend notes that archaeological evidence suggests that the Donatist cathedral was not burned down. Frend, *Donatist*, 296.

30. Fage, *History*, 487. Gregory, *Ep.* 1.72, 1.82, 11.33, and 111.32.

10

Summary of North African Christianity

THROUGHOUT THIS WORK, I have asked this question or a variation of it: "Where is the church?" This question serves as a focal point to place the Donatist controversy within the tradition of North African writers and to show that this tradition reflected the views of many North African Christians from the second to the fifth century. Keeping this question in mind, I have also sought to trace the idea of how "church" was defined in North African Christianity through its understanding of baptism, persecution, and martyrdom in the writing of various African fathers, starting with Tertullian who laid the foundation for what was to follow. I contend that once we understand the Africans' idea of the church and its relationship to key doctrines, such as baptism, martyrdom, and the concept of *origo*, then we can fully appreciate why the majority of Christians in North Africa were attracted to Donatist teaching: because the Donatists continued to build upon the African traditions that were articulated by Tertullian and continued by their beloved hero and martyr Saint Cyprian. This is not to say that the Donatist Church ceased to evolve or that it was as monolithic as Augustine seems to suggest. On the contrary, there were nuances in their teachings that were specific to each writer and period. For example, I have shown that Tertullian, Cyprian, and Petilian all made reference to the concept of *origo*, and I have also demonstrated how each writer adapted its use to meet the challenges of his particular period.

Tertullian used this concept with the "rule of faith" and thus demonstrated that the gnostics and other heretics were outside the church because they could not prove any connection to the apostles or the apostles' teaching. Cyprian also used this concept but adjusted it to suit his purposes. Because of the severe divisions caused by the Decian persecution, Cyprian used the concept of *origo* or the concepts of *unitas* and *origo* together as a way of explaining the unity of the church and its proper source. He considered the Novatianists or other schismatics deplorable because they both tried to introduce another source into the church and challenged his authority. He also connected the concept of *origo* with the episcopate. Thus, Cyprian emphasized how the apostle Peter was the source or the starting point on which the church was built. This served him well, because he could then claim that this power was not given to Peter alone but to all the apostles and every rightful bishop after him, including Cyprian himself. Hence for Cyprian the question "Where is the church?" was answered by emphasizing that first and foremost the church is where the bishop is and that the bishop is God's anointed filled with the Holy Spirit to lead and guide the body.

Cyprian thus did an excellent job of bringing out the authority of the bishop and his importance in governing the church. However, because of the serious internal problems resulting from Decian's persecution, Cyprian was forced on account of doctrinal conflicts to expand the question to ask "Where is the church and who are its members?" It is on this point that Cyprian influenced future generations of African Christians, for Cyprian claimed that schismatics and heretics were basically in the same category: they were outside the bounds of the true church and must be rebaptized. Moreover, if a sacrament was performed outside the bounds of the true church, it was meaningless. So Cyprian and other African bishops considered baptism (or rebaptism, as it was called by their opponents) absolutely necessary for those who had received what purported to be the sacrament outside what they believed to be the true church.

When Bishop Miltiades of Rome criticized Bishop Donatus of Carthage for rebaptizing heretics, the latter was not acting in defiance of a sister church but was simply following the tradition of African bishops. When Constantine supported Caecilian's group against Donatus, he was in fact supporting the minority point of view in Africa. By interfering in the affairs of the North African churches and supporting Caecilian as rightful bishop, Constantine unintentionally exacerbated the situation. This played into the hands of the Donatists, as it allowed them to claim that the state and the Catholics were their persecutors. Drake has shown, however, that Constantine's main concern at the time was to maintain peace and stability throughout the empire, and like emperors before him, he wanted the united prayers and support of the religious community, now the Christians. However, the schism between the North African churches forced Constantine to choose between competing parties. For practical and religious reasons, Constantine favored Caecilian's group. This brought resistance from the Donatists, and for a brief period Constantine sought to suppress them. To Constantine's credit, however, he did not continue the suppression of the Donatists beyond 321 but allowed both groups to worship freely for the remainder of his reign. This is important, because it supports my thesis that the majority of African Christians—when not forced—believed that the group led by Donatus represented the true church in North Africa. I also argue, citing comments from the conference at Carthage, that the claim of being the "true church" was made in regard to Africa only. Contrary to what Augustine repeatedly claimed, the Donatists did acknowledge other churches outside of their homeland, but in Africa they insisted they were the true Catholic Church.

The Donatists were certainly the more popular church in North Africa and as a consequence had to eventually accept the fact that they were not a small persecuted church of the martyrs. By 347, the Donatists were the majority church with their own bishops, ecclesiastical discipline, and manner of worship.[1] Moreover, the realization that they were the majority church influenced Donatist theology. Bishop Parmenian was creative in addressing this situation. Through his teaching on the *dotes* (gifts) present in the true church he was able to acknowledge sinners within the Donatist fold while continuing to insist on separation from the Catholics. With this advance in Donatist theology, the Donatists were able to take a major rhetorical weapon away from the Catholics. Bishop Parmenian skillfully acknowledged sinners among Donatists (thus denying that they thought themselves a pure or perfect church) while simultaneously maintaining that they were the true church.

I have also argued that Augustine did not fully appreciate the Donatist teaching on baptism and their connection to Cyprian. As a result, the Donatists were not at all persuaded by his rhetoric. Part of the

---

1. Challenging Yvette Dual's contention that the Donatists were a small insignificant group, Frend states: "Throughout the fourth century, however, the Donatist Church was the majority church of North African Christians. Modern attempts to diminish its importance and play it down as 'le clan donatiste' fly in the face of the evidence." Frend, "Donatus," 626. In this article, Frend shows why Jerome claimed that the Donatists had deceived all of Africa. Despite this article and Frend's book on the Donatist Church, some scholars have not yet moved beyond earlier sterotypes.

problem is that Augustine's conversion experience happened in Milan under the influence of Ambrose; hence, his outlook on Christianity was more Roman than African. Augustine may have finally realized this towards the end of his life, for in his *Retractiones* he admits that he was not an expert in the Donatist theology of baptism. I suggest this was not an expression of modesty but in fact what Augustine came to realize. Nonetheless, Augustine's obsession with defeating the Donatists caused him to do exactly what Petilian accused him of: to use his tongue to induce persecution of the Donatists. By 405, Augustine and his colleagues had influenced Emperor Honorius to implement another Edict of Unity, but this time with anti-heresy provisions against the Donatists. And in 411, the Donatists were ordered to a conference for the purpose of being condemned. Nonetheless, the Donatist bishops made every effort to put up a good fight so that future readers of the conference of 411 could decide for themselves the nature and location of the true church in North Africa.

Bibliography

PRIMARY SOURCES AND TRANSLATIONS

Actes de la Conférence de Carthage en 411. Edited and translated by Serge Lancel. SC 194, 195, 224 and 373. Paris: Cerf, 1972–1991.

The Apostolic Fathers. Translated by J. B. Lightfoot and J. R. Harmer. 2 vols. Edited and revised by Michael W. Holmes. Grand Rapids: Baker, 1989, 1990.

Augustine. "The Anti-Donatist Writings." Translated by J. R. King. The Nicene and Post-Nicene Fathers 4. Edited by Philip Schaff. Edinburgh: T. & T. Clark, 1872. Reprint, Grand Rapids: Eerdmans, 1989.

————. *The Confessions.* Translated by Maria Boulding. Hyde Park: New City, 2002.

————. "Contra litteras Petiliani Libri Tres." Translated by G. Finaert. Bibliothéque Augustinienne, series 3, vol. 3. In *Œuvres de saint augustin 30:Traités anti-donatistes.* Paris: de Brouwer, 1967.

————. "The Retractations." Translated by Mary Inez Bogan. The Fathers of the Church 60. Washington, DC: The Catholic University of America, 1968.

————. *Scripta Contra Donatistas.* Edited by M. Perschenis. Corpus Scriptorum Ecclesiasticorum Latinorum, vols. 51–53. Leipzig: Freytag, 1908.

Cyprian. *Acta Proconsularia Sancti Cypriani.* Translated by Herbert Musurillo. In *The Acts of the Christian Martyrs.* Oxford: Clardendon, 1972.

————. *De Lapsis and De Ecclesiae Catholicae Unitate.* Translated by and edited by Maurice Bévenot. Oxford: Clarendon, 1971.

————. "Fathers of the Third Century: Hippolytus, Cyprian, Caius, Novatian." Translated by Ernest Wallis. The Ante-Nicene Fathers 5. 1886. Reprint, Grand Rapids: Eerdmans, 1990.

————. *S. Thasci Caecili Cypriani Opera Omnia.* Edited by Hartel. Corpus scriptorum ecclesiasticorum Latinorum, 3. Vienna, 1871.

————. "The Epistles of Cyprian." Translated by Ernest Wallis. The Ante Nicene Fathers 5. 1886. Reprint, Grand Rapids: Eerdmans, 1975.

————. "The Letters of St. Cyprian." Vols. 1 and 2: Letters 1–54. Translated by G. W. Clarke. Ancient Christian Writers. New York: Newman, 1984, 1986, 1989.

————. "The Life and Passion of Cyprian." By Pontius the Deacon. The Ante-Nicene Fathers 5. Edited by Philip Schaff. 1886. Reprint, Grand Rapids: T. & T. Clark, 1990.

————. "Epistulae, 1–57." Corpus Christianorum. Series Latina, 3B. Edited by G. F. Diercks. Turnholt: Brepols, 1994.

————. "Epistulae 58–81." Corpus Christianorum. Series Latina PB, 3C. Edited by G. F. Diercks. Turholt: Brepols, 1996.

————. Epistularium: Prolegomena-Indices. Corpus Christianorum. Series Latina, 3D. Edited by G. F. Diercks. Turnholt: Brepols, 1999.

Des origines à la mort de Constance II (303-361). Edited by Jean Louis Maier. Vol. 1, *Le dossier du Donatisme.* Berlin: Gottfried Wilhelm Leibniz, 1987.

Donatist Martyr Stories: The Church in Conflict in Roman North Africa. Translated by Maureen A. Tilley. Liverpool: Liverpool University Press, 1996.

Eusebius. *The Ecclesiatical History and The Martyrs of Palestine.* 2 vols. Edited by H. J. Lawlor and J. E. L. Oulton. 1928. Reprint, London, 1954.

————. *The Ecclesiastical History of Eusebius Pamphilus.* Translated by Christian Frederick Cruse. Grand Rapids: Baker, 1990.

Lactantius. "Writings." Translated by William Fletcher. The Ante-Nicene Fathers 7. Edited by Alexander Roberts and James Donaldson. Buffalo: The Christian Literature Company, 1886.

Livy. *The War with Hannibal: Books 21–30 of the History of Rome from its Foundation.* Translated by Aubrey de Sélincourt. London: Penguin, 1965.

————. *History of Rome: Books 5–7.* Translated by B. O. Foster. Cambridge: Harvard University Press, 1924.

————. *History of Rome: Books 28–30.* Translated by Frank Gardner Moore. Cambridge: Harvard University Press, 1949.

————. *The Early History of Rome: Books 1–5 of the Ab Urbe Condita.* Translated by B. O. Foster. Reprint, New York: Barnes & Noble, 2005.

Marcellinus, Ammianus. 3 vols. Translated by John C. Rolfe. Loeb Classical Library. London: Harvard University Press, 1940. Reprint, 1956.

Optatus. *Against the Donatists.* Translated by Mark Edwards. Liverpool: Liverpool University Press, 1997.

————. *Traité contre les donatistes.* Vols. 1 and 2. Translated by Mireille Labrousse. Paris: Cerf, 1995.

Passio Sanctarum Perpetuae et Felicitatis. The Martyrdom of Saints Perpetua and Felicitas. Translated by Hebert Musurillo. In *The Acts of the Christian Martyrs.* Oxford: Claredon, 1972.

Passio Sanctarum Scillitanorum. The Acts of the Scillitan Martyrs. Translated by Hebert Musurillo. In *The Acts of the Christain Martyrs.* Oxford: Clarendon, 1972.

Patrologiae Cursus completus, Series Latina. Edited by Jacques Migne. 221 vols. Paris: 1844–1894.

Polybius. *The Rise of the Roman Empire.* Translated by Ian Scott -Kilvert. London: Penguin, 1979

Porphyry. *Porphyry's Against the Christians: The Literary Remains.* Translated by R. Joseph Hoffman. Amherst: Prometheus, 1994.

Tertullian. *Apologeticus and De spectaculis,* Translated by T. R. Glover. Loeb Classical Library. Cambridge: Harvard University Press, 1931. Reprint, 1984.

————. "Apology, Spectacles, To the Martyrs." Edited by Robert D. Sider. In *Christian and Pagans in the Roman Empire: The Witness of Tertullian.* Washington, DC: The Catholic University Press of America, 2001.

————. "Latin Christianity: Its Founder, Tertullian." Translated by Alexander Roberts and James Donaldson. The Ante Nicene Fathers 3. London: SPCK, 1885. Reprint, 1964.

————. "Tertulliani ad martyres." Edited by A. Gerlo, 1954. In *The Tertullian Project* at http:// www.tertullian.org/works/ad-martyras.htm.

————. *Tertullian's Homily On Baptism.* Edited and translated by Ernest Evans. London: S.P.C.K.,1964.

———. "The Writing of Tertullian Voume 1." Translated by Alexander Roberts and James Donaldson. Ante-Nicene Christian Library 11. London: T. & T. Clark, 1889.

Tyconius. *The Book of Rules.* Translated by William S. Babcock. Atlanta: Scholars, 1989.

WORKS CITED

Barnes, Timothy David. *Tertullian: A Historical and Literary Study.* Oxford: Clarendon, 1971.

Brent, Allen. *Cyprian and Roman Carthage.* Cambridge: Cambridge University Press, 2010.

Bright, Pamela. *The Book of Rules of Tyconius: Its Purpose and Inner Logic.* Notre Dame: University of Notre Dame Press, 1988.

Brisson, J. P. *Autonomisme et christianisme dans l' Afrique romaine de Septime Sévère à l' invasion vandale.* Paris: De Boccard, 1958.

Burns, J. Patout Jr. *Cyprian The Bishop.* New York: Routledge, 2002.

Chapman, D. J. "Donatus the Great and Donatus of Casae Nigrae." *Revue Bénédictine* 26 (1990) 13–23.

Courcelle, Pierre Paul. *Recherches sur les "Confessions" de saint Augustin.* Paris: E. de Boccard, 1968.

Drake, H. A. *Constantine and the Bishops: The Politics of Intolerance.* Baltimore: John Hopkins University Press, 2000.

Dunn, Geoffrey D. *Tertullian.* New York: Routledge, 2004.

Elliott, Thomas George. *The Christianity of Constantine the Great.* Scranton: University of Scranton Press, 1996.

Evans, Robert. *One And Holy: The Church in Latin Patristic Thought.* London: SPCK, 1972.

Fage, J. D., and Roland Oliver, editors. *The Cambridge History of Africa.* 8 vols. Cambridge: Cambridge University Press, 1975–1988.

Fox, Robin Lane. *Pagans and Christians.* New York: Knopf, 1986.

Florovsky, Georges. *Bible, Church, Tradition: An Eastern Orthodox View.* Belmont: Nordland, 1972.

Frend, W. H. C. *The Donatist Church: A Movement of Protest in Roman North Africa.* Oxford: Clarendon, 1952. Reprint, 1970.

———. "Donatus 'paene totam Africam decepit' How?" *Journal of Ecclesiastical History* 48 (1997) 611–27.

———. "The Gnostic-Manichaean Tradition in Roman North Africa." *Journal of Ecclesiastical History* 4 (1954) 13–26.

———. "Manichaeism in the Struggle Between St. Augustine and Petilian of Constantine." *Augustinus Magister* 2 (1954) 859–66.

———. *Martyrdom and Persecution in the Early Church: A Study of a Conflict from the Maccabees to Donatus.* Oxford: Basil Blackwell, 1965.

Gaddis, Michael. *There is No Crime for Those Who Have Christ: Religious Violence in the Christian Roman Empire.* Berkeley: University of California Press, 2005.

Heffernan, Thomas J., and James E. Shelton. "Paradisus in carcere: The Vocabulary of Imprisonment and the Theology of Martyrdom in the Passio Sanctarum Perpetuae et Felicitatis." *Journal of Early Christian Studies* 14.2 (2006) 141–55.

Hermanowicz, Erika T. *Possidius of Calama: A Study of the North African Episcopate.* Oxford: Oxford University Press, 2008.

Hinchliff, Peter. *Cyprian and the Unity of the Christian Church*. London: G. Chapman, 1974.

Lewis. Gordon. "Violence in the Name of Christ: The Significance of Augustine's Donatist Controversy for Today." *Journal of the Evangelical Theological Society*. 14 (1971) 103–10.

Merdinger, J. E. *Rome and the African Church in the Time of St. Augustine*. New Haven and London: Yale University Press, 1997.

Miles, Margaret. "African Spirituality: Forms, Meanings and Expressions." In *African Spirituality: Forms, Meanings, and Expressions,* edited by Jacob K. Olupona, World Spirituality: An Encyclopedic History of the Religious Quest 3, 350–71. New York: Crossroad, 2000.

Mokhtar, G. *General History of Africa: II Ancient Civilizations of Africa*. Berkeley: University of California Press, 1980.

Monceaux, Paul. *Histoire littéraire de l' Afrique chrétienne depuis les origines jusqu'à l'invasion arabe.* 7 vols. Paris: Leroux, 1901–1923. Reprint, Brussels: Civilisation et Culture, 1963.

Pagels, Elaine. *Adam, Eve, and the Serpent*. New York: Vintage, 1989.

Perkins, Judith. *The Suffering Self: Pain and Narrative Representation in the Early Christian Era*. New York: Routledge, 1995.

Rives, J. B. *Religion and Authority in Roman Carthage From Augustus to Constantine*. Oxford: Oxford University Press, 1995.

Sacks, David. *A Dictionary of the Ancient Greek World*. Oxford: Oxford University Press, 1995.

Schindler, A. "L'histoire du Donatisme considérée du point de vue de sa propre théologie." *Studia Patristica* 17.3 (1976) 1306–1315.

Sider, Robert Dick. *Christian and Pagan in the Roman Empire: The Witness of Tertullian*. Washington, DC: The Catholic University of America Press, 2001.

Stark, Rodney. *The Rise of Christianity: How the Obscure, Marginal Jesus Movement Became the Dominant Religious Force in the Western World in a Few Centuries*. San Francisco: Harper Collins, 1997.

Tilley, Maureen. *The Bible in Christian North Africa: The Donatist World*. Minneapolis: Fortress, 1997.

———. "Dilatory Donatists or Procrastinating Catholics: The Trial at the Conference of Carthage." *Church History* 60 (1991) 7–19.

———. "From Separatist Sect to Majority Church: The Ecclesiologies of Parmenian and Tyconius." *Studia Patristica* 33 (1997) 260–65.

Wilhite, David E. *Tertullian the African: An Anthropological Reading of Tertullian's Context and Identities*. Berlin: Walter de Gruyter, 2007.

Willis, Geoffrey G. *Saint Augustine and the Donatist Controversy*. London: SPCK, 1950.

Zoch, Paul A. *Ancient Rome: An Introductory History*. Norman: University of Oklahoma Press, 1998.